To MACllister

David Taylor is one of a handful of independent veterinary consultants to zoos, marine-lands and safari parks. At a moment's notice he and his partner must be prepared to fly anywhere in the world to the aid of sick and injured animals. His patient can be a malevolent tiger, a frostbitten killer whale or a giant panda with stomach ulcers. His adventures are always fast-moving and brimming with good humour.

He is the author of five books. These are the basis for a major television drama series about his life and work. David Taylor is a Fellow of the Royal College of Veterinary Surgeons and of the Zoological Society of London.

ZOOVET

The World of a Wildlife Vet

Zoovet

The World of a Wildlife Vet

DAVID TAYLOR

London
UNWIN PAPERBACKS
Boston   Sydney

First published in Great Britain by George Allen & Unwin 1976
First published by Unwin Paperbacks 1984

UNWIN® PAPERBACKS
40 Museum Street, London WC1A 1LU, UK

Unwin Paperbacks
Park Lane, Hemel Hempstead, Herts HP2 4TE, UK

George Allen & Unwin Australia Pty Ltd
8 Napier Street, North Sydney, NSW 2060, Australia

British Library Cataloguing in Publication Data

Taylor, David, 1934–
    Zoovet.
1. Veterinary medicine   2. Zoological gardens
I. Title
636.089′092′4   SF745
ISBN 0–04–925024–8

Typeset in 11 on 13 point Baskerville by Nene Phototypesetters Ltd
and printed in Great Britain
by Cox and Wyman Ltd, Reading

To my parents,
Frank and Marian Taylor
of Rochdale

One

Slowly, painfully, Chota the elephant shuffled through the damp, grey Manchester morning towards the zoo dispensary. Her back was arched and her spine stood out like the keel of an upturned boat. Her ribs heaved distinctly under the tight dry skin where the weeks of chronic pain had stripped the flesh from her bones. Each leg was advanced reluctantly only a few inches at a time, accompanied by a low grunt and a small puff of steaming breath from the tip of her trunk. Moving for Chota was a continuing agony.

Twenty years before, as a six-month-old baby, she had been taken from her mother and put into a small stockade near Calcutta with a large number of other young elephants, most of them well under the age of weaning. Here she had waited several months for the arrival of the European animal dealers who would come to buy new stock. Tended by ragged elephantmen who fed the youngsters on watered cow's milk and balls of damp rice, some of the young elephants had died from attacks of acute enteritis or from strangulating hernias of their navels. The others, including Chota, had survived and had seemed to thrive well enough. But rice balls and watery milk are no adequate substitute for the rich sustenance that flows from the twin teats between the forelegs of a mother elephant. The balance of minerals, the content of calcium and phosphorus and vitamins, was wrong and, although nothing could be seen from the outside nor would be for many years, the delicately forming structures of the baby elephant's joints suffered serious damage. Nineteen years of careful, well-balanced feeding in the zoo at Manchester could not repair the

1

original faults in the growing tissues, and eventually the dread signs of osteoarthritis had appeared.

After all that time the rice balls of India had led to small holes appearing in the smooth, oiled bearing surfaces of Chota's fetlock joints. The holes had grown larger, the springy covering of tough cartilage had been eaten away, and the bare bones of the upper and lower parts of the joints had begun to grind remorselessly away on one another. First the elephant had shown stiffness, then lameness, and then a profound disinclination to move at all because of the pain. It was no use her shifting the weight from one leg to another: all the joints were as bad and each one was carrying around one ton of weight on its raw surfaces. Chota knew the worst pain of all was when she had to rise to her feet after reclining. Then the poor hind fetlocks had to take two tons of pressure each. It was too much. She became unwilling to lie down and because of the constant pain her standing sleep was fitful and increasingly brief. Chota became exhausted and began to lose weight.

The vet had done everything possible to relieve the pain and slow down the disease, but this was 1950 and the new range of anti-arthritic drugs, the cortico-steroids, the injectable analgesics and phenylbutazone were not readily available for veterinary use. Chota had flatly refused to eat powdered aspirin in her food for the dose was one third of a pound of the stuff and even in molasses or jam the taste could not be disguised. The elephant keeper had tried to drench the aspirin into Chota by standing on a chair and pouring the white suspension into her mouth from a watering can but to no avail. Her podgy pink tongue had curled up and blocked the narrow space at the back of her mouth and not a drop had got through. The thick skin around the inflamed joints had dispersed much of the heat from poultices which were applied and there had been no sign of any easing. So, after much discussion, the zoo director and the veterinary surgeon had decided on euthanasia.

Chota's last day of life was my introduction to zoo animal medicine as a student. Newly arrived at University, I was spending my first half-term 'seeing practice' with the firm of vets who looked after Belle Vue Zoo, Manchester, and the first visit on my first day travelling round with the senior partner was to the zoo to put an end to Chota's misery. The main room of the dispensary had been cleared of everything except a small instrument table by the time we arrived. Matt Kelly, the head keeper, and his deputy were waiting for us, subdued and tense. Matt had known Chota for many years and was an expert in the handling and management of elephants. On summer days he had supervised the crowds of children who had taken rides round the grounds on Chota and her friend, Mary. Nobody said very much as we unloaded the equipment from the vet's car: syringes, needles, large bottles of barbiturate.

When everything was prepared Matt gave the order for Chota to be brought in. The elephant keeper led and coaxed her forward. The keeper had been at the zoo for over twenty years. He had taken care of the baby when she arrived shivering, hairy and wide-eyed on a cold December morning after a long sea passage from Bombay. He had slept with her in the elephant house during her first few weeks in her new home, made up her gruel, selected the best fruit for her and kept over-indulgent visitors and other members of the staff at bay. He had brushed her daily, oiled her skin once a week, cleared her of ticks and lice and seen her through bouts of colic and diarrhoea and constipation. He had manicured her toenails to stop cracking, hardened the soles of her feet with formaldehyde to avoid rot and fished irritating hay awns out of her ears. The young elephant knew that he always took the chill off her drinking water and that he kept boiled sweets, with the wrappings off, in his left-hand coat pocket. Soon after her arrival, she had burnt herself by pressing too hard against a radiator and the keeper had sat up all night with her, sponging the burn with a soothing lotion. She had learned to trust and respect him. By means of the boiled sweets he had taught her to perform some simple tricks. She could tell by the tone of his

3

voice when he was annoyed and he sometimes admonished her by slapping her or tapping her with the round end of a walking stick. The spiked elephant stick, its sharpened point and hook hidden in gaily coloured feathers, an instrument used viciously in some circus quarters, was something she knew nothing about.

Chota shambled to a stop in the middle of the dispensary. Her keeper toyed nervously with her ear and spoke quietly to her in the pidgin Indian that elephant keepers use. Looking up into her gentle grey eyes, I wondered how one could examine and treat such gigantic creatures. If I had known how many more sick and diseased elephants I was one day going to deal with, I should have found the prospect unnerving.

The vet had finished his preparations. The keeper rubbed the animal's right ear and murmured closely to her, while Matt Kelly took the left ear and flapped it forwards. With pressure from his thumb he raised one of the great blood vessels that run close to the skin along the back of the ear. With a quick jab the vet inserted a needle into the vein. Chota made a little squeal but did not move. Blood flowed from the needle and the vet attached a tube leading to a large bottle of barbiturate solution. Raising the bottle as high as he could above his head, he allowed the liquid to flow slowly in the vein. Over three pints of the anaesthetic would be required: the days when I would knock down a fully grown bull elephant with two c.c.'s of a drug simply popped under the skin were yet to come. Minutes passed and the liquid continued to flow. Chota stood quietly gazing down at us. She began to blink her eyelids and a tear ran slowly down her cheek from the corner of one eye. Then she sighed and her eyelids drooped progressively until they were almost closed.

'Don't anyone stand too close to her now,' said the vet. 'She'll go down any time.'

We backed away and the vet stood warily, the rubber tube between bottle and needle fully extended. Very gently, Chota began to sway backwards and forwards. Suddenly she buckled at the knees, pitched forwards, and with a tired groan slipped

4

over onto her side. The needle was still in the vein and the liquid flowed on. Another bottle, the fourth, was connected to the rubber tube. Now Chota was completely unconscious, free at last from the throbbing fire in her limbs. The elephant keeper, deathly pale, slipped quietly out of the door.

We stood and watched as the anaesthetised elephant continued to breathe steadily. The fifth and final pint of barbiturate was connected to the tube and I took over from the vet the strain of holding the bottle as high as possible to give maximum flow. I stood looking down at Chota's great head. More tears were trickling out of the one closed eyelid that I could see and making their way erratically across the dusty cheek. The only noise was the bubbling of air into the bottle as the syrupy liquid slowly disappeared down the tube. When all the drug had been used the needle was withdrawn from the ear and we stood round Chota's body, watching. Still the mighty chest rose and fell with a regular rhythm. The vet bent down and flicked at Chota's eyelid with his finger: the long luscious eyelashes twitched. There was still some reflex there. Crouching down he pushed his hand into her mouth and tugged at the slippery ball of her tongue. The pink ball resisted, quivering and contracting under his grasp. When he took his hand away it pulled itself back like a great pink toad retiring beneath a stone. Half an hour passed, an hour. Still Chota breathed gently on in oblivion.

The vet was talking quietly to Matt Kelly. 'This is the trouble with barbiturates. They're very slow in a big animal like this, especially with the strongest solution we've got containing only one grain in a c.c. At least it's absolutely painless. Wouldn't have fancied shooting her.' I remembered hearing that a veterinary student had recently been killed in Scotland by a bullet ricocheting from the skull of a zoo elephant that was being destroyed.

'I think we'd better try to hurry things up a bit.' The vet had other cases in the zoo to attend to. 'Let's try some carbon monoxide.'

A keeper came in through the door pushing a motor bike. Behind him two others struggled under the weight of a heavy folded tarpaulin. Chota breathed steadily on as the tarpaulin was unfolded and arranged over her body until she was completely covered by it. The black heap in the middle of the dispensary floor had none of the features of an elephant. It was more like a pile of sand sheeted as a protection against the rain. Now a tube was attached to the exhaust pipe of the motor bike which was propped up on its stand close to the invisible elephant's head. The free end of the tube was pushed under the tarpaulin and the engine of the bike was kicked into life. The metallic crackle of the machine rattled round the bare room. As a blue haze began to fill the air, we left the dispensary. Matt wedged the double doors open and arranged for a keeper to stay on guard outside so that no-one would enter while we went round other parts of the zoo.

An hour later we returned to the dispensary. Chota still breathed on, though with barely perceptible movements of her chest. Her reflexes were much weaker and her tongue was an unpleasant dark colour. It was arranged that the gassing should continue and that we should come back to the zoo in the afternoon to perform a post-mortem. The elephant keeper, utterly distraught, had been sent home.

When we had finished the day's rounds we drove back to Manchester and reached the zoo just after its closing time. The offices and animal houses were dark, the staff had left, but the dispensary was brightly lit. As we went in through the doors I stopped in astonishment. The room had been transformed into a slaughterhouse. The remains of Chota, massive pink, red and grey chunks, lay in piles on the floor or hung from hooks. The air was thick with steam and the strong, acrid smell of dead elephant. Knackermen had been called in to dismember the carcass and they were arranging the organs and limbs in ordered groups for inspection by the vet. Heart and lungs here, head there, intestines unravelled and displayed in neat zig-zags. It was an ogre's kitchen. Hosepipes swept blood and

6

excrement continually towards the drains. The men chatted cheerfully and deftly honed their knives with steels that they carried in wooden holsters hanging from their belts. An elephant was something very unusual for them. They were used to the daily harvest of cattle carcasses, bloated through overeating new grass or withered from the tubercle bacillus. This was something out of the ordinary with lots of interest and scope for jests. It was fresh and they would be paid good overtime.

It was my first post-mortem on a large animal, and as awesome in its way as my first sight of the Jungfrau or the interior of King's College chapel. Of the indifference with which the knackermen, full of oaths and wisecracks, tossed the great floppy ears about, I did not know what to think. The vet poked and prodded around in the piles of steaming flesh. With a scalpel he sliced into organs of interest, split blood vessels and scraped away slime.

'See how the lungs are strapped to the ribs with all this white gristle?' he asked me. 'It looks like very severe pleurisy.'

At the time I had not even begun to study pathology and knew nothing of the ways in which diseased tissues change, but I saw how the lungs were indeed covered by thick fibrous bands which attached them firmly to the inside of the chest wall.

'That's where lots of people make mistakes when doing elephant p.m.'s,' he continued. 'They think they've found something and diagnose pleurisy, when in actual fact it's part of an elephant's normal architecture. Unique but normal.'

Years later I found that old records of elephant autopsies did indeed frequently report the presence of 'chronic pleurisy', and on one occasion this error led to a case of anthrax in an elephant which died in a British zoo being missed. The virulent disease spread horrifically when the carcass, apart from the 'pleurisy'-affected areas, was fed to other carnivorous inmates of the zoo.

The vet cut into the joint cavities of poor Chota's limbs.

7

Severing the powerful ligaments and tough capsules, he cracked open bearing surfaces and revealed their ravaged features. There it was: angry deep ulcers worming their way through the cartilage, blood and clumps of cells like rice grains mixed with the joint oil. The fetlocks of each leg showed the same degree of damage. Matt Kelly had seen many elephants develop the progressive signs of arthritis, and it had always ended this way. He shook his head grimly as he watched the vet probe into the joints with the scalpel, following the ulcers like worm holes deep into the tender bone.

'It was just as well,' he murmured. 'She must have suffered horribly.'

At the end of the post-mortem we drove silently home. I would write up the case for the report that a student had to present after seeing practice. Surely, I thought, there must be better ways of doings things for suffering elephants in the future. How many more of these magnificent creatures would I see brought down so sadly? What would it be like to handle a case of disease in a large zoo animal on one's own responsibility? But of one thing I was utterly certain: I was determined that when I had qualified I would concentrate on the health problems of exotic animals.

Two

My desire to work with animals stretches back further than my memory. As a small child I never considered for a moment becoming anything other than a veterinary surgeon. Animals rather than people interested me, and the mysteries of disease in animals were particularly fascinating. The little blobs of fluffy fungus that grew with unfailing regularity on each year's batch of tadpoles in the jam jars that I kept in my bedroom, the itchy bald patches that sometimes afflicted second-rate specimens of white mice begged from the testing room at the gasworks, the hedgehogs found torpid and dying for no apparent reason on the playing fields, the pathetic cast ewes inexplicably unable to struggle to their feet, so often seen during walks over the moors round my home – these were the things that fired my ambition. Animal disease seemed then, and still does, somehow 'purer' than human medicine. Matters are not complicated by the fantasies or mendacities of the patient, although I did learn in general practice that owners can exhibit hypochondria on behalf of their pets, that pet poodles or scrapyard alsatians frequently reflect the temperaments of their masters, that bears can develop troublesome haemorrhoids, and that goats accustomed to experiencing symptoms of the 'bends' during repeated experimental 'dives' in pressure tanks soon learn to fake the typical clinical picture in order to receive rewards of food, just like the human malingerer.

Even as a boy my fascination was more with wild animals than domestic ones. Toads, bats, hedgehogs, lizards – these creatures still interest and excite me more powerfully than pedigree dogs or thoroughbred horses. I still consider it a privilege to touch and handle an undomesticated animal. Close contact with the warm hair, the skin, the chunky muscle of wild animals, even the touch of a walrus or a rhino or a lion, gives me a physical thrill. How I envied the older boys at Manchester Grammar School when I first entered the Biology Department and heard how they had been given octopus to dissect in the practical scholarship examinations for University. One bright lad had been given his oral test on a strange skull that was shaped just like a bird's but was as big as a pig's. We new boys, struggling with the innards of the frog and dogfish, marvelled at the strange object and puzzled over what it could be and what fiendish traps might lie ahead for us when it was our turn to sit the examinations. It was my first meeting with a creature that was to figure largely in my life twenty years later, for the skull was that of a bottle-nosed dolphin.

After studying veterinary medicine at Glasgow University for five years, I toyed with the idea of going to Kenya to research in sleeping sickness of animals and similar protozoal diseases. At the last minute I decided to stay in Glasgow and do a course in comparative pathology. It was a wise move, for much of the investigation of disease in exotic animals depends on the proper handling, examination and interpretation of specimens of diseased tissue, on microscopic work, and on the bacteriological testing of samples of blood, pus and other liquids. After one year of this I went back to my home town of Rochdale to join a general practice dealing with a wide range of large and small animals. Most importantly, it was the firm with which I had 'seen practice' and which had as a client the large zoo at Belle Vue in Manchester. As well as being able to work with exotic animals I would receive a sound grounding in all aspects of general veterinary work.

A young vet could not have practised anywhere better. We had everything: rugged moorland sheep farms, cattle farms, riding schools, prison farms, greyhound kennels, and all the dogs and cats and budgerigars that teem in the cobbled streets, shabby avenues and high-rise flats of the cotton towns of Greater Manchester. Stitching and cutting, injecting and lancing, struggling to replace the prolapsed womb of a cow on a Pennine farm at three o'clock on a blizzard-swept February morning, digging up rotten carcasses of pigs to obtain pancreas glands for swine fever tests, pinning stray tomcats' fractured limbs just after closing time on Saturday nights, delicately removing fatty tumours as big as plums from parrots with doting owners and beaks that could slice steel – it was the finest training.

The art of surgery is the same in a peke or a panda, a donkey or a zebra. The more I learnt about handling animal tissues, opening and closing limbs and organs, using drugs and handling violent, awkward and terrified animals and owners, the more I would be able to do for similar problems in wild animals. Surgery is after all just needlework on living, bleeding flesh. The more you learn to cut and stitch confidently and neatly, the more practice you have, the better you become. Likewise, it is by his work on the obstetric problems of cows, dogs and horses that a vet must acquire his skill in correcting the baby's position manually within the womb, and in performing Caesarean operations. There just are not enough cases of complicated birth occurring in giraffes or polar bears for him to refine his techniques by working on those species alone.

As well as the collection in the Manchester Zoo, I came across a growing number of privately owned exotica during my years in Rochdale. Knowing that I was interested in the problems of these offbeat pets, and often unable to find a vet in their locality who was willing to examine the creature or knew the first thing about treating it, the owners would bring their beloved snakes or monitor lizards or bush babies for miles. Some owners were more ambitious. There was a spinster lady in Bury who favoured slow lorises, and a family in Higher Blackley who had no televison set but sat instead at night around the built-in herpetarium in the lounge and watched their collection of diamond-backed rattlesnakes and twelve-foot boa constrictors dispose of white rats. Then there was the clumsy idiot who let a spitting cobra escape from its tank and make off angrily for the darkness of the machinery behind my surgery refrigerator.

Something Ray Legge, the director of the Manchester Zoo, once said about it being 'understandably the usual practice' for zoos to call in doctors of human medicine when their great apes were ill struck a nerve in me. Of course it was understandable in some ways. Great apes – gorillas, orang-utans and chimpanzees – do resemble man in many respects and have similar disease problems, but doctors never seemed to treat cases of disease in animals quite seriously enough. We had had lots of co-operation from medical workers at places such as Manchester University, but when it came down to it they were interested mainly in their narrow speciality, getting the specimens, the samples they could work on. The ophthalmologists were keen to get specimens for their collections of retinas or lenses, the anaesthetists were happy to try out new hypnotics, the virologists wanted blood serum and more blood serum for their comparative studies. All well and good, but none of them was interested or cared deeply enough for the animals as individuals, as patients with problems to be cured. To some vets and doctors, treating exotic animals may be a welcome change from routine work, something to tell the wife about tonight, but to me it was and is completely serious.

I decided that it was time for someone in the veterinary profession, not using animals just for research purposes, to show that the medicine of great apes was a serious veterinary field. I would study for the Fellowship of the Royal College of Veterinary Surgeons in Diseases of Zoo Primates. On my half-days off I worked at the great ape house in Belle Vue or pored over books in the Medical Library at the University. At weekends I travelled round the British zoos such as Twycross and Regent's Park which have extensive primate collections. I made the most of every photographer's monkey or circus chimp that came my way during surgery hours. Eventually, after a long written examination in Glasgow and a practical and oral examination at Edinburgh Zoo, I obtained my FRCVS. To celebrate, my wife, Shelagh, and I bought a Japanese bronze of a mother tortoise and her brood and I went off to my first big international symposium on zoo animal diseases in Austria. I had made up my mind to leave general practice and see if I could earn a living purely from exotic animals.

If I was going to do it I must do it properly. No more dogs or cats or pigs or cattle. I would set up an office at my home just outside Rochdale and accept nothing but calls concerning exotic animal cases. It was a gamble. Like all vets I am bound by rules of professional conduct so it was not possible to advertise my presence, and snakes and monkeys and parrots are much, much thinner on the ground in Lancashire than are dogs and ponies. Nor is there much in the way of fees when treating sore eyes in a child's three-inch terrapin or replacing the prolapsed anus of a six-inch grass snake.

First of all I had to learn much more about zoo animals and in particular about the other side of the fence, the non-veterinary aspects. It is fine for a vet to dash into a zoo and advise on this or that problem and then disappear, but what about the many other facets of zoo keeping and maintenance? I needed to know more about the economics of purchasing, breeding and feeding stock, the education of staff, the political set-up within a zoo company, questions of transport and housing and public relations. I needed to know especially how all these things bear upon the welfare of the animal inmates. So I became curator-cum-veterinary officer for Flamingo Park Zoo in Yorkshire and the other zoos owned by the same company. Apart from handling an ever-increasing number of exotic animals, I found myself thrust into the strange new world of non-veterinary zoo work. On the one hand I was veterinary officer responsible for the health of killer whales, tigers and performing parrots and on the other hand, wearing my curator's cap, I had rapidly to master the day to day

13

problems of staff management, food buying, cleaning and sweeping and public relations. I was also in charge of first aid and the toilet block!

Most important of all, it was through Flamingo Park that I was first able to study some of the most exciting zoo exhibits. One of the first zoos to bring dolphins into Europe, Flamingo Park sent me all over the world to learn more about the habits and special requirements of sea mammals and other rare animals. I began to travel extensively – to Greenland to see musk ox and walrus (having equipped myself with the latest Arctic survival clothing from a shop behind Manchester Cathedral, I arrived in Narssarssuaq in Greenland one November day to find the Eskimos tiptoeing through the snow in winklepickers and suede jackets), to all the major zoos of Europe, to the marinelands of Canada and the United States and, most important of all, to the United States Navy base at Point Mugu in California. It was from the vets of the US Navy's undersea warfare research department that I learned the basic techniques of examining dolphins and whales and sealions, and it was at Point Mugu that I experienced the thrill of taking my first blood sample from a dolphin – a dolphin that the Americans were training to plant limpet mines on enemy submarines.

Gradually, my interest in primate diseases was overtaken by the medical problems of cetaceans, the whale and dolphin family. As with general zoo work, it was essential to learn every bit of the booming dolphinarium and marineland business. With the skilled dolphin fishermen of the Gulf of Mexico I went out hunting for the nimble and intelligent bottle-nosed dolphins. In boats that could touch 65 mph and turn on a sixpence at full speed, and with spotter planes overhead searching for suitable schools of dolphins, I learned how to handle the newly caught animals, how to stop a baby dolphin once aboard from committing suicide by literally holding its breath, and how to tell the difference between a shark and a dolphin tangled in the nets and out of sight deep beneath the

14

ocean. The techniques of shipping these delicate animals across continents and over oceans had to be mastered, as had the problems of overheating, of cracking skin, of bed sores, of parasites, mercury poisoning and pneumonia. So much and so different from the surgery in Rochdale and the lectures and demonstrations at University.

Andrew Greenwood, my partner, joined me in 1972, having been a student seeing practice with me while still at Cambridge. Intensely interested in exotic animal diseases and particularly in marine mammals and in falconry, after qualifying he had researched for the Royal Navy in pathological problems associated with diving. Increasingly during that time he had stood in and done locums for me while I was globetrotting. We travel at the drop of a hat all over the world to wild animals in need of help. Our bags contain changes of clothes and toilet equipment, certain key drugs and medicines which might be unobtainable overseas, a few basic instruments and a selection of sample bottles, tubes and blood specimen needles. The office is full of airline timetables, lists of hotels in Timbuktu and Toronto, maps of the German autobahn system and receipts from credit card companies. Good communications are essential – each of our cars is fitted with a radio telephone linked to a private nationwide network and sometimes when out of our vehicles we carry personal radio pagers. Above all the work is satisfying and exciting and we are proud to be doing it. It is all simply summed up for me in the two words of our original telegraphic address: ZOOVET ROCHDALE.

Three

Right up to the beginning of the sixties exotic animal medicine was in a sorry state, lagging far behind the new developments in diagnosis and treatment that were revolutionising domestic animal practice. The key problem was the difficulty of getting to grips with dangerous and hyperexcitable animals and rendering them safely immobile or unconscious for surgery, close examination or the delivery of young. Two things were essential above all else: effective, well-tolerated anaesthetics for a vast range of species with differing anatomies and physiological functions and a good means of administering them. Of course we had the barbiturates which worked well if injected into a vein, but how to persuade a pain-wracked rhino to stand still while you raise his jugular with the pressure of one thumb and squeeze in an intravenous needle with the other? New gases such as halothane were superseding ether and chloroform, but what persuades a bolshy sealion to inhale deep of the soporific vapour in the face mask when, as an accomplished deep-sea diver, he is used to holding his breath for ten minutes at a time? Drugs which in capsule or tablet form bring speedy oblivion to a human with an empty stomach tended to get lost in the hundredweights of digesting food and churning liquid inside a hippo's or elephant's stomach. Or they produced bizarre responses, as when I tried one reliable human tranquilliser by mouth on bison. Instead of making the animals calm and sleepy, it whipped them into an amazing state of sexual frenzy, transforming even the most decrepit old males into bellowing satyrs that dashed about mounting every female they could lay their hooves on.

Quieting a dangerous or nervous patient was not the only problem in anaesthetising exotic animals. Nine years after Chota's tragic end in the dispensary at Belle Vue Zoo, I was called to attend her old friend, Mary, who had been suffering from increasingly severe attacks of toothache. Elephants have a peculiar tooth arrangement with a system of continual replacement throughout their lifetime of the grinding molars. The teeth develop from buds at one end of a groove in the jaw, move forwards into use as they grow, and then fall out to be replaced by others coming along the groove behind them. This process sometimes hits snags. A tooth jams instead of falling out cleanly and the animal shows all the signs of tenderness and irritation in the mouth that humans would associate with an impacted wisdom tooth. Mary's problem was one stage worse than this: she had developed an abscess at the base of a tooth root in the lower jaw. The abscess enlarged and caused severe pain within the unyielding confines of the bony jaw. Mary became irritable and grumpy. She ate little other than soft over-ripe bananas. She drooled saliva more than usual and would open her mouth for inspection only with great reluctance.

When I was first called to examine her I asked the keeper to persuade Mary to open her mouth. Eventually, after lots of soothing talk, I could put my hand inside. Feeling about in an elephants's mouth is not the least hazardous of veterinary procedures. There is not much room, and it is easy to find one's fingers being pushed by the strong muscular tongue between the grinding surfaces of the teeth, a most excruciating experience. When I tapped the infected molar with the back of my knuckle, Mary pulled back, beat me lustily about the head with her trunk and screeched like a pig. A root abscess: normally one would extract the tooth and all would be well. At least that was how things went in other animals, but in an elephant it was quite a different matter. The tooth in question was firmly embedded in the jaw and, like all elephant teeth, had multiple curved roots which sweep deep down into the jawbone and interweave intricately with the bony tissue around them.

Pulling, even with giant forceps, was out of the question and so was elevating, the flicking out of a tooth by means of a lever-like instrument. I decided to try medical treatment instead, to destroy the abscess by injections of antibiotics and to relieve pain by injectable analgesics.

The snag with this course is that the trouble tends to flare up again some weeks or months later. Sure enough the injections produced rapid disappearance of all symptoms and within a day Mary was her own amenable self again. Two or three weeks later the zoo rang up to say that Mary was beginning to show the same symptoms again but this time the pain was so bad that she was banging her head against the wall. I drove down at once to Manchester and sure enough a very forlorn Mary was having trouble again with an abscess under the same tooth. The drug injections quickly put matters right and the following day the elephant had stopped the head-banging.

Over the next six months Mary had four more attacks of toothache involving the same tooth root and each attack was more severe and lasted longer than the one before. The headbanging became the principal symptom. Mary would stand for hours close to the wall of the elephant house, deliberately rocking on her ankles and crashing the affected side of her head against the brickwork with a regular, dull, horrible thud that could be heard two hundred yards away. She had knocked the paint off a large area of the wall and loosened the pointing between the bricks. The last attack was the worst. Mary refused all food but stood night and day against the wall, seeking to counter the aching focus in her jaw by temporarily distracting the throbbing nerves as one ton of head jarred into the brickwork. It was terrible to listen to and unpleasant to watch: she was bruising and cutting the skin on the side of her face and she was becoming ill-tempered and unpredictable to handle. What was more, the wall was defin-itely no immovable object assailed by an irresistible force. It was beginning to bulge outwards, many bricks were loose, and the zoo director feared that the structure of the building was now at serious risk. We had to do something more positive. The tooth causing all the trouble would have to come out.

It was clear that the only way to remove the offending molar was to perform a major operation on the jaw. The gum along the side of the tooth root would have to be flapped up, the thick covering plate of bone would then be chipped away and the tooth with its roots intact could be teased, cajoled and manoeuvred sideways out of the jaw. This would mean a long period under general anaesthetic: a shot of local as performed by the dentist, or even a nerve block, the numbing of the nerve to the tooth by surrounding it with local anaesthetic at some point on its path back towards the brain, would not be feasible. The area of tissue involved was too large and complicated and the animal was in far too agitated a state. Anyway it would be impossible to do the necessary work unless she was lying down with her head still.

The problem was that at this time, the late fifties, there was no really suitable general anaesthetic available for the elephant. Major operations on the elephant had rarely been performed. Local anaesthetic was used for minor matters but otherwise it had been a question of tying the poor creature down with chains and hobbles and using the crudest of methods. Giving chloroform or ether was virtually impossible; barbiturates had to be given intravenously in ridiculously large doses, had a nasty knack of damaging the veins and tissues round about where they were injected and depressed breathing seriously, while chloral hydrate, the old stand-by of horse practitioners, was so disgustingly bitter when given in water that an animal would need to be stopped from drinking for three or four days before it would accept the doctored liquid. I decided to look into the possibility of using a new and promising drug which I had been using for two or three years on other exotic creatures.

Giving Mary a stiff dose of pain-killer and antibiotics to relieve the situation, I announced that we would operate on her the following day and that suitable preparations should be

19

made. Then I went home to consider further the matter of anaesthesia in this, my first case of major surgery on the elephant.

The new drug, phencyclidine, had been the first important breakthrough in modern zoo animal anaesthesia. It was highly concentrated, formed a stable solution which had no annoying tendency to go off, and could produce its effects when given by any route including by injection under the skin, by mouth or in a flying dart. Its taste was not too bitter, so that when used to spike the fruit drinks or milk of those discerning and wide-awake customers, the great apes, it usually went down unnoticed. There were disadvantages, too. The dose was calculated on body weight, and once it was administered there was no way of neutralising its effects, which wore off gradually over a number of hours. Some animals such as polar bears were easily overdosed with the stuff, and I noticed how little phencyclidine they needed to knock them flat out compared with brown or Himalayan black bears. Wolves, the first animals on which I had ever used the chemical and the tranquillising gun, frequently developed alarming convulsions when unconscious under phencyclidine. The drug had proved to be unsuitable for horses and I had discovered to my dismay that it had serious untoward effects in zebra: instead of anaesthetising an animal which had broken out of its pen and could only be dosed by means of a flying dart containing phencyclidine, the drug produced an alarming degree of excitement and distress which persisted for hours. But in monkeys and apes, the big cats and some other carnivores it was superb. We never saw any signs of the long-lasting sexual stimulant effects or burning sensations of the fingertips and toes which humans treated with the drug had reported, although big cats under phencyclidine anaesthesia do regularly extend and contract their claws.

For Mary's operation phencyclidine was the best drug I had at the time. Checking that evening through my library I found one or two reports of its previous use on elephants, but details were scanty. What was suitable as an experimental dose in the African bush where elephants were plentiful was not necessarily right for Mary, a valuable and much loved animal in a city zoo in the industrial north of England. I had to get the dose right. Another problem is estimating the weight of an animal such as Mary. My usual practice is to walk the animal or take it in a lorry to a public weighbridge, but the toothache had made Mary crotchety and unco-operative and I could not risk taking her out of the elephant house. If an animal cannot actually be weighed I take the average of three estimates made by myself and two other people accustomed to working with animals, which is what I had to do in Mary's case. With the small amount of information which I had accumulated I was able to calculate a dose for the following morning. Certain nagging problems remained: how long would the anaesthetic last and what would be the cumulative effect of any further doses once she was down? What awkward physiological changes would several hours' unconsciousness produce in the ponderous creature? How was I to ensure that she went down with her bad tooth uppermost? It is not easy to turn a four and a half ton elephant when she is collapsed unconscious like a great pile of coal.

The next morning I was up early. My first call was to the local ironmongers. Dental instruments for human or ordinary veterinary use are far too puny for the granite-hard teeth of an elephant and the thick, resilient bone in which they are embedded. What I needed was a set of high-quality, all-metal masonry chisels. The ironmonger produced exactly what I wanted, a set of tough tungsten-edged tools specially intended for punching holes in hard stone. When I explained what they were for, the shopkeeper said he would sell them to me at trademan's price.

'After all,' he said, 'you're using them for your trade, I suppose. Never thought I'd find myself selling surgical instruments!'

At the zoo I found Mary suffering considerably from the diseased tooth. The pain-killing drug had worn off and she

21

was in a black mood. As I entered her quarters she glowered down at me and shuffled agitatedly around, whisking and flailing her trunk. It was going to be difficult keeping her still enough even for the normally simple under-skin injection of phencyclidine. I decided to leave all the instruments outside until she was anaesthetised. How she would go down and whether, during the few seconds that the anaesthetic first affected her brain cells, she would feel dizzy and become alarmed, I did not know. But I remembered having cases of horses run amok during the first stages of barbiturate dosage, with disastrous effects on the surrounding and carefully sterilised equipment, and I was not taking any chances.

Matt Kelly solved the problem of keeping Mary still for a second or two while I gave her the dope. Mary had one great weakness – an unbridled appetite for custard pies, the open, nutmeg-sprinkled, Lancashire variety. Even though the tooth-ache had quenched her desire for more conventional foods, Matt guessed that she would still be quite unable to resist these delicacies and he sent up to the zoo restaurant for some. Sure enough, when a keeper appeared with a box full of the newly baked golden pastries, the demeanour of the miserable animal immediately changed. Her black mood became, well, charcoal-grey, she stopped roaming irritably about and proceeded with obvious enjoyment to roll the custards one after another into her mouth, carefully avoiding the offending left side of her jaw. While she was thus engaged I slapped three times on her rump with the flat of my hand and then, when she was accustomed to the contact, slapped her again with equal force but this time with a three-inch needle held between my fingers. She did not feel a thing as I connected the syringe full of anaesthetic to the needle and pressed the plunger. It was in. I had begun the general anaesthesia of my first elephant.

Mary continued to consume the last of the custard pies, still standing calmly as we silently watched her. The elephant's soft munching was the only sound to be heard. Now I was going to be faced with the answers to the questions with which

22

my mind was racing. What was the effect of the drug going to be? Was my dose adequate or perhaps even too large? Had my needle squirted it deep into a layer of fat where its absorption would be greatly delayed and the effect minimised? A minute passed. Mary cleared the last flakes of pie pastry from her lips and looked at Matt for more. No signs of grogginess. At what time should I consider giving another dose, I wondered, clenching my fists. How would a second injection act in relation to the first? What would the cumulative effects be? Suppose the first effects on Mary were indeed to make her feel dizzy and alarmed. What if she ran amok while still sufficiently conscious to stay on her feet? For a moment I almost wished myself back in the everyday vet's world of anaesthetising dogs with fractured legs and ponies for castration.

Two minutes passed, then five. Suddenly, as if chilled by a gust of icy air, Mary began to tremble. Her knees buckled and she sagged down on legs of jelly. With a drowsy sigh and a boom as her leathery side hit the thick carpet of straw on the floor, she crashed over. She was flat out with the operation site and the bad tooth fortuitously uppermost. Matt and Mr Legge, the zoo director, positioned her legs and trunk as comfortably as they could and I checked her breathing and the working of the massive heart with my stethoscope. The operation was under way.

The peeling back of a large flap of gum over the root area took only a few minutes and the bleeding was very quickly controlled with forceps. Then began the slow business of chipping away the bone. It was fantastically hard. I struck the sharp chisels with a heavy metal mallet, working to a guideline painted on the bone in purple antiseptic dye. I was working naked from the waist up, as I prefer to do during prolonged large animal operations, particularly in warm animal houses. The effort was making my arms ache and the sweat streamed down my face and chest. Hordes of little red mites from the straw saw it as their duty to climb aboard and stroll about my body, making me itch annoyingly. Bit by bit, but far slower

23

than anticipated, I chipped my pathway along the jawbone. It was so hard that the jarring as the mallet and chisel rebounded from the dense tissue began to numb my hands. Mary remained perfectly unconscious. From time to time I stopped my chiselling to examine her pulse and breathing – so far all was well.

After two hours I had at last broken through the jawbone right along the line I had marked. Then, using a strong stainless steel bone 'pin' rather like a small crowbar, I levered the plate of bone off. There below it was the whole of the troublesome molar's complex root system. Like an iceberg, there was far more of the tooth below the surface than protruded above the gum, and the roots were still hideously intertwined with a lace-work of bony bridges. On and on I chipped, gradually freeing the broad, curved root branches. With my crowbar I tested my progress now and again by attempting to lever the great tooth outwards. Still it remained firmly implanted. After four hours I could at last see the inflamed area on the root that was the cause of all our problems. It was not much to look at: just a pinkish-yellow blob about the size of a pea. Another hour passed and then, as I tried levering outwards yet again, there was a loud cracking noise and the largest tooth I have ever extracted heeled over and fell out of the jaw with a thud.

From now on it was plain sailing: replace the plate of bone, fill the gaping hole in the gum (it was as big as a house brick) with a four-pound ball of sterilized dental wax, and stitch up. As I began the last lap, replacing the gum flap, I noticed that the colour of the gum was not as bright pink in colour as it had been. The colour was now distinctly tinged with lilac. I hurriedly completed the last knots in the catgut and sat back exhausted on my haunches. The colour change in the gum had diluted some of the elation in finishing the job. Now to attend to the animal's general condition and protect it from post-operative complications. Mary still lay dreaming on her side. Her reflexes were becoming a bit stronger. First I checked the

24

heart and lungs again. Her heart was thumping strongly but faster now. As I listened to her lungs, with the stethoscope placed on the uppermost part of her chest, all sounded normal.

Then, faintly, from far away, I heard the deep rumble of a new sound, a dull bubbling noise far below the healthy swoosh of air in and out of the lung nearest to me. I went round to the other side of the animal and knelt down, pushing my stethoscope hard into the tight space between the underneath side of the chest and the floor. I could not get very far in but the bubbling noise was distinct, rather like a cauldron of jam gently boiling. I knew what was beginning to happen. The immense weight of the animal pressing down on the lung nearest to the floor was interfering severely with the flow of air and blood through the vital tissues, and fluid was collecting in the underneath lung. It is something to be watched for in all animals lying on their sides under anaesthetic and it can usually be prevented by turning the animal frequently from side to side.

'Let's get her over as quickly as possible,' I said. 'I don't like the sound of the right lung.'

Matt and his keepers hurried to attach ropes to Mary's feet and to push planks as levers beneath the bulging belly. Everyone pushed or pulled. Keepers braced themselves with their feet against walls and their backs wedged beneath Mary's legs.

Gradually we raised her until she was lying on her backbone with all four feet in the air. Then we let her down gently on the other side. I gave injections of heart and lung stimulants and drugs against shock and infection. The bubbling noise was now less noticeable in the right lung but, to my horror, I detected the first sounds of it in the other lung. Mary had been down under anaesthetic for too long. Although she was beginning to rouse, she had a long way to go and I had no way of speeding up the process. The lungs were becoming fatigued. We were in trouble. Mary was beginning to drown.

Her breathing became steadily more laboured and abnormal. She was more restless and moved her legs and trunk erratically. She even tried to raise her head a few inches from the ground. The unpleasant sounds in both lungs increased and, more ominously, some areas of the lung tissue became silent: they had filled completely with liquid and there was no longer any movement of air through them. An oxygen cylinder was set up and the gas was fed by tube under a sheet placed over Mary's head. For a moment I saw again, as if in a nightmare, Chota's tarpaulin-covered body as I had seen it on my first visit to this very zoo. Although now the tube which led under the sheet carried not deadly carbon monoxide but life-giving oxygen, it was beginning to look as though the end result would be the same, for Mary's breathing was steadily weakening. If only I could have reversed the effects of the injected anaesthetic! A full return to consciousness and the ability to stand and move would soon have restored good circulation in the chest.

Mary's colour was changing for the worse. The gums were now grey-blue with only a hint of pink. The respiration was weaker and seemed more laboured. The interval between breaths became agonisingly longer.

'Stand next to me and we'll try artificial respiration,' I said to Matt, who was standing glum and tight-lipped. 'Both together we'll get on and off the chest to see if our weight can compress the ribs.'

Simultaneously we both jumped onto the rounded grey chest of the recumbent giant. The rib cage sank a little. We immediately jumped off again. There was a slight expansion of the chest, but it was impossible to tell how much air had been sucked in. We repeated the process. On, off, on, off: at five-second intervals we jumped with all our weight onto Mary's chest. We tried jumping up and down on the chest itself. Our exertions produced some wheezing as small amounts of air were forced in and out but it was not enough. I stopped and listened again with the stethoscope. The lungs

26

were in dire trouble, with fluid building up, and the heart was beginning to fail fast. I gave more injections, more circulation stimulant and a chemical to give a kick in the pants to the centre in the brain that controls breathing. It was no good. Five minutes later Mary stopped breathing altogether and the heart-beats faded away fainter and fainter until I could hear them no longer. Mary, the most famous of Manchester Zoo's elephants and voted by schoolchildren their favourite animal in the park, was dead.

The autopsy on Mary confirmed that the long operation under phencyclidine had produced serious fluid build-up in the lungs with a resulting fatal lack of oxygen and heart failure. The zoo director and I had a meeting with the Board to report on Mary's loss. It was miserable explaining how my technique, up to date as it was, just had not been safe enough for a long operation on an elephant. I told the Board that if another elephant developed the same problem as Mary on the following day I would have to do the same again, using the same anaesthetic. It would be so until someone developed a new way of tackling anaesthesia in the elephant.

Four

Phencyclidine was the first breakthrough in the anaesthesia of most exotic species, and the invention of the dart-gun solved almost completely the problem of getting the anaesthetic to the patient while the vet stayed well out of range of its claws, teeth, hooves or horns. Gradually, pharmaceutical firms began to develop new experimental chemicals. They did the laboratory work; it was up to me to test the drugs in real live wild animals in the field. The bottles of prototype drugs with labels bearing only code numbers arrived regularly on my desk, accompanied by all available data concerning their effects on cats, rabbits, dogs or pigs. I could not risk losing or injuring any animals, but the new drugs were badly needed and very cautiously I began to try them out on my zoo patients. Bit by bit, feeling my way with the dosage levels, varying the strengths of the injected solutions, ringing the changes on 'cocktails' made up of mixtures of drugs, and working with emergency cases in a widening circle of species, I began to find means of sedating almost all zoo animals safely and quickly to any desired level. The process continued until eventually there were only two species which I found particularly difficult to anaesthetise without worry, the sealion and the giraffe.

In other ways, too, there have been dramatic advances in zoo medicine over the past twenty-five years. I doubt, for example, whether I shall ever again see an elephant destroyed because of osteo-arthritis. Powerful X-ray machines can easily penetrate the tree-trunks that are an elephant's legs and pick out the first signs of disease. With ingenious fine fibre-optic tubes carrying lights and lenses I can actually look inside the joint

28

cavities and inspect the diseased surfaces. Although I still use poultices of freshly-brewed infusions of comfrey leaves, the herbal 'knitbone' therapy so popular among the older Lancashire people of the Pennines where I was born, on the legs of elephants, now I can reinforce such time-honoured methods with injection into the joint of modern cortico-steroids, the feeding of tasteless new anti-arthritic drugs in the food, and courses of healing and pain-relieving ultrasonics.

Chota and Mary, the Manchester elephants, both died because the drugs, equipment and techniques available could not cope with the special problems posed by their massive bulk. Because of its sheer size the elephant is the species which illustrates most clearly and dramatically the developments in zoo medicine, and it was through his elephants that I first met Billy Smart junior, when he brought his troupe to Manchester for the Christmas circus. The animals were quartered in stables behind the King's Hall in Belle Vue. One of the elephants had begun to show signs of arthritis identical to those displayed by the ill-fated Chota. The pain had affected her normally placid temperament and on the evening before my visit she had attacked and beaten a circus elephant keeper so badly that he had had to be taken to hospital for emergency removal of a ruptured spleen. The keeper had made things much worse for himself by going into the elephant lines late at night after returning somewhat the worse for an evening's drinking. Elephants, like many other animals, are very sensitive to changes in the manner and mood of those who attend them. Reeking of beer, with perhaps a louder voice and rougher style of speech than normal, and probably moving on his feet less deliberately and calmly than usual, the keeper was not recognised as its friend by the aching elephant which had settled down in its usual place for the night. The man was on his own and could easily have been killed.

It is always risky as a stranger to move among elephants unaccompanied. Elephants look after one another. They have special friends and mates among their companions from whom, in sickness or health, they are usually inseparable. As I move between two elephants to prod or feel at something they will tend to press together, making me a filling inside a great living elephant sandwich. It can be difficult to sqeeze out, and I usually find myself dropping down and wriggling out between the forest of massive legs. If I inject one elephant its protective neighbour will often reach out and clout me sternly with its trunk or, worse, if it has tusks, lunge out with the ivory points at my body. One has to keep talking gently but firmly, to move steadily and decisively and to bear gifts: Polo mints are very well received.

The Smarts' elephant was indeed in the early stages of arthritis, but after a fortnight's treatment with the new arsenal of anti-arthritic drugs that were just becoming available, the animal was back to normal. When the troupe left Manchester at the end of the Christmas season she was walking normally and showed no sign of joint damage. Billy Smart seemed pleased with the result and said that he would contact me when next he had problems with the elephants, his special love. A few months later I was in Cyprus on holiday with my family when we saw a large photograph on a Cypriot magazine cover displayed in a bookshop in Nicosia. It showed Billy Smart standing in a car-wash with an elephant which was being shampooed in this modern and rather novel way. Prominently visible on the thigh of the animal was a lump the size of a cricket ball. An abscess or a tumour, I remarked to Shelagh, my wife. We had no way of knowing when the photograph had been taken. Perhaps it was something which had been dealt with long ago. I soon forgot about it.

When I returned to England I found myself busy with elephants again, this time a group of baby African elephants which had been brought to Flamingo Park in Yorkshire. They were a wild and riotous bunch, fourteen in number and all about four feet high. They had come straight from the African bush and although youngsters were fearless and aggressive. They had to be examined carefully: some had weak and bent ankle joints, others I suspected of being ruptured at the navels. But as soon as I approached closely to inspect them, they flared their ear flaps and charged at me, squealing angrily. One young male took such a dislike to my attentions that he chased me across the elephant house and beat me against the concrete wall with a blow of his broad bony forehead. I literally saw stars. It was obviously going to be necessary to use anaesthetic on these young tearaways if I was to have any chance of giving them a thorough check-up.

First supplies of a new anaesthetic drug called M99 were just coming in. Good reports about it were being published by vets working with wildlife in Africa and I had already found it first-class for knocking out deer and wildebeest, but this would be my first attempt to anaesthetise an elephant since the sad affair of Mary. M99 is a drug of the morphine family but thousands of times stronger. It is effective in minute doses, particularly in elephants, and most important of all it can be instantly neutralised by an antidote drug. So efficient is the antidote that animals return from anaesthesia to complete normality within seconds and without any grogginess or hangover. For the young African elephants at Flamingo Park I decided to use M99 even though at that time it was costing approximately £480,000 per pound. Very little, just a few milligrammes, would be required for each animal, I was assured.

Each young elephant was injected by a flying dart fired from a special gas-powered rifle. One to two minutes after the dart had struck an elephant's plump buttocks, the animal would sink quietly without any sign of alarm or dizziness to the ground. The medical inspection over, I slipped a small dose of antidote into the ear vein and within two minutes the animal was on its feet, eating food and glaring suspiciously at me once more. It looked as if M99 was going to be the answer to the terrible problem of doping elephants.

Two months later the telephone rang. It was Billy Smart junior. Gilda, one of his elephant troupe, was having trouble with a strange lump on her hind leg. Apparently the lump, the size of a large apple, had been there for about a year, but over the past three weeks it had begun to grow very rapidly and was now as big as a melon. I drove down to Leicester where Smart's Circus was playing and went into the elephant lines. Sure enough, Gilda was the elephant I had seen in the photograph in Cyprus. The swelling in her leg was hard but apparently painless. Its base was deep below the skin in the great thigh muscles.

'What do you think it is?' asked Billy. He had had years of experience with elephants and with the abscesses, cysts and skin diseases which are commonly seen in the species, but he had never seen a lump behaving like this one.

'It doesn't look like an abscess or cyst to me,' I replied, exploring the consistency and shape of the thing with my fingers. 'I think it's a tumour.'

Billy had trained the elephants himself and thanks to his remarkable rapport with them I was able to push a special biopsy needle deep into the lump in order to sample the tissue without the animal reacting or making a fuss. Billy just stood at Gilda's head talking firmly and kindly to her and stroking her trunk while she gazed devotedly down at him. The speck of flesh on the end of the biopsy needle was sent to the laboratory for microscopic examination. A few days later the result came back that it was a tumour, with areas of cancerous change. A major operation to remove it was imperative.

This time the anaesthetic would be M99. My experiences with it in the African elephants and other animals had impressed me, but I travelled down to Leicester again with a slight feeling of apprehension. Everything had been beautifully arranged in the elephant tent for the operation. Deep straw had been piled on the ground and covered with new canvas sheeting. The other elephants had been moved far away to the other end of the tent, where they stood with necks bent and eyes popping inquisitively as they watched with an air of disapproval what we were preparing to do to their companion. Gilda had not been given any solid food for twelve hours prior to the operation and was grumbling a bit about this as she was led onto the canvas sheets. She tried to grab bits of straw from the bedding as an illicit snack and became irritable when Billy Smart stopped her.

'I think I'll bring Burma over to stand by her,' said Billy. 'It will give her more confidence.'

Burma is the gorgeous old matriarch of Smart's Circus elephants. The first elephant that the famous Billy Smart himself bought, very big, looking always uniquely old and wise, she is the most intelligent, gentle and patient elephant I have ever met. She is just the sort of companion you want next to you in time of trouble, reliable, a rock. The Smart family worship her and see that at Christmas, weddings and other festivals, or if she looks a little peeky, she receives a bottle or two of her favourite tipple, neat Bisquit de Bouche cognac. The presence of Burma near a nervous, distraught or ailing elephant always seems to bring calm and confidence to the sufferer. I have often been glad of her help when treating sick or injured animals in the Smarts' winter quarters at Winkfield.

Burma came and stood impassively and quietly next to Gilda, who seemed immediately reassured. It was not necessary even to drop the anaesthetised elephant onto the floor. Billy simply gave Gilda the command to lie down (this is just one of the advantages of working with circus as opposed to zoo elephants) and the elephant obediently lay down with the tumorous leg uppermost. I could almost hear Burma murmur in approval. It was easy to inject just two c.c.'s of the M99 solution painlessly into Gilda's ear vein, and within half a minute and without any problems she passed from conscious rest into a deep and satisfactory sleep. It took me about an hour and a half to cut out the great growth. Although elephant skin is tough, it is nothing like as thick and awkward to work with as, say, rhinoceros skin, and ordinary scalpels cut through it with

33

the greatest of ease. The time-consuming part was the tying-off of all the blood vessels that supplied the hidden depths of the tumour.

When at last the mass had been totally dissected out (I had been at great pains not to leave behind even one particle that might multiply into another tumour) there was left a gaping hole in the thigh which had to be closed. The skin was virtually impossible to slide across the hole, the gap was so large and I had been forced to remove such a great expanse of skin. For a moment I was frightened. The hole had to be closed, but how? Using double lengths of the thickest stitch material I had, a sort of plaited nylon fishing line with a breaking strain of 250 lb, I inserted 'relaxation sutures', which go through the skin far behind the wound edges and take the main strain. I put dozens of them in place and gradually tightened them. Slowly the wound began to close. As the first relaxation sutures went slack I tightened them and reinforced with more. At last it was finished. The hole was sealed, although the operation site looked like a spider's web of interweaving green nylon. I prayed it would be strong enough to withstand the pressures when Gilda moved about. After tidying up the wound I filled my syringe with the anaesthetic antidote, injected it into the ear vein and looked at my watch. Thirty seconds later Gilda sighed deeply, switched her trunk and rolled her eyes. Then she heaved herself over onto her brisket and with a little grunt rose to her feet. No wobbling, no dizziness. Gilda looked round, touched trunks briefly with Burma and then grabbed a tuft of straw protruding from beneath the canvas. She stuffed it hungrily into her mouth. The stitches held.

There was no further trouble with Gilda and her growth. The last sign of it was the faint white scar which could just be detected the following Christmas when I sat with Shelagh and watched Billy Smart's Circus on television. The audience in the big top and the millions of television viewers undoubtedly enjoyed the scintillating and colourful display as the elephants carried clowns and glamorous girls about the ring. But the glimpse of that thin and fading line on the prancing grey hams of an elephant made me the proudest person on earth that Boxing Day afternoon.

Five

The only bit of advice on treating exotic animals that students were given when I was at University was that wallabies go dotty over Fox's glacier mints! My Professor of Surgery, Sir William Weipers, told us how he had discovered this fact when called in to a case of frostbite on the tails of wallabies kept on the lawns of some Scottish country house. Wallabies, a highly-strung species liable to drop dead from shock if harassed or handled roughly, are like most other zoo animals in that they must be approached gently, patiently and bearing gifts of sweetmeats. It is amazing what can be done at the back end of a correctly approached and undoped animal as long as it is being fed something it fancies at the front end. At Belle Vue Zoo a special brown bread used to be baked daily for the animals. Almost all of them, whether herbivore, carnivore or something in between, adored it, and while a keeper supplied one chunk of loaf after another to the drooling camel or bison or brown bear, I would be taking temperatures or injecting at the rear.

Before the days of reliable and compact sedatives for zoo animals Matt Kelly, head keeper at Manchester, had showed me some of the knack of coming to grips with his animals. From him I learned how to catch a lion's or a leopard's tail as it sauntered by the bars of the cage and then to drop down so that the tail was bent over the edge of the cage floor. With the indignant lion roaring and pulling horizontally, and me using my weight vertically on the bit I was holding, the edge of the floor took most of the pressure and I could hold a fully grown big cat with his bottom up against the bars in a perfect position for injecting. From Matt I learned how to hypnotise a crocodile by turning it onto its back and stroking its belly, and how to baffle a bloody-minded parrot, bent on a mouthful of human finger, by a neat piece of kung-fu that leaves the astonished bird flat on its back and safely immobilised in less time than it takes to tell.

The learned journals are full of papers on the pathology and physiology of aardvarks and axolotls but the vital scraps of information that make life easy for the zoo vet, and save wear and tear on fingers and horn-holes in various parts of the anatomy, have to be gathered from experienced men like Matt Kelly. From Matt I learned how to root out an absconding porcupine that has installed itself under a fairground carousel and is gleefully gnawing away at the works, and how to negotiate with a monkey that has stolen a packet of razor blades and, like some Indian fakir, is packing the lethal leaves of steel into its cheek pouches. A gazelle or antelope, released suddenly from its carrying crate, may dash headlong into the walls or netting surrounding its paddock and injure its head and limbs terribly, even breaking its neck and dying instantly: I had seen it happen with zebra. Matt showed me how to use double-doored crates so that animals could be made to emerge rear ends first. This stops the frantic dash and allows them to get their bearings as they turn. I may never know whether some of the things Matt told me will work in practice. What to do when an enraged and highly dangerous male chimpanzee charges at you? Matt swore that he had once been in this position and that quick as a flash he had dropped his trousers and stuck his bottom in the air to impersonate a chimp in the submission posture. It worked. The chimpanzee reacted predictably to this signal which says 'OK, I give in. You're the greatest' and checked his attack. I hope that if I am ever in a similar predicament my zipper does not stick!

Some of the things I saw at zoos and circuses were not for learning, like the chimpanzees' tea party whose animals were not just as good as gold, they were almost automata. The audience marvelled at the obedience of the little apes and smiled as the trainer fondled their hairy heads. It was all in the fondling. The man showed me his thumbnail which had been allowed to grow long and then filed into a vicious point. It was strong and horny and he used it with cruel skill to gouge and twist the sensitive flaps of the chimpanzee's ears. It was really a display of brutal sleight of hand carried on in full view of the public. I was to find that this method of controlling chimps by their delicate ears was commonplace in the world of chimpanzee training: even mature specimens were subdued by the agony of a quickly applied hold.

Although many circus animals are trained without cruelty, there are still terrible black spots. You will find them in the smaller, tatty circuses and menageries if you can penetrate the closed, suspicious, obstructive world behind the scenes. It is a world skilled in repelling outsiders and deceiving RSPCA inspectors and, most important, able to move on if trouble is brewing. At first hand I have seen bears encouraged to move from travelling box to circus ring by lighted newspapers thrust underneath them, and I have heard the regular, sickening thuds as a chained African elephant was beaten systematically with bamboo rods by two keepers to break it by literally torturing it until it collapsed. The most repellent feature of the process was the calm clinical way in which the keepers administered the beating. It was a job, just like grooming, which called for a repetitive movement for long periods of time. No anger, no emotion, just a boring job of beating. Of course when the police arrived the men were indeed grooming the elephant. Bamboo rods applied with all a man's might across the rib-cage of an elephant leave no marks.

One hard-bitten old lion trainer showed me his method for giving pills to lions. 'Watch this, young fella,' he said, running the big male lion into the barred tunnel between ring and travelling cage. 'Quicker and better than all your dart-guns and powders on the meat.'

When the lion was halfway down the tunnel the trainer slipped a board between the bars in front of it and a similar

38

one behind to make a simple treatment cage. He picked up a crowbar and a bottle of aspirins, shoved the crowbar through the bars and cracked it hard down on the animal's head. The lion was at his mercy, unable to back away or turn around. It roared thunderously, opening its jaws and raising its head. The lion trainer dropped in a couple of aspirins. Down they went and the lion closed its mouth. The trainer hit the lion's skull again. The sound was sharp and revolting, the clang of metal on bone. The lion roared again in frantic impotence. Two more aspirins went in.

'See? How's that, eh?' said the trainer proudly. 'No problem, eh?'

'Bloody horrible,' I replied. He would never understand, never.

Sadly there will always be some showman who is prepared to use inhumane methods to create a new crowd puller. At one marineland in the United States the high spot of the show was a water-skiing elephant. I was there on the day that the elephant was persuaded by much use of the feathered spike to mount a pair of specially constructed giant skis. The rolling anxious eyes and the shrill trumpeting showed clearly that the elephant was an unwilling amphibian – so unwilling that once in position it was chained to the skis and the chains were secured, not by padlocks as is usual when tethering elephants, but by heavy nuts and bolts. To the applause of the crowd and the smooth spiel of the loudspeakers the motor boat towing the skiing elephant pulled away onto the smooth water of the lake. The animal waved its trunk and seemed to hang back on its chains. The skis tipped up at the front as the boat accelerated.

'Look at Herbie go, folks!' enthused the loudspeakers. 'My, he's sure enjoying himself?'

The skis were supported beneath by large buoyancy chambers so Herbie did not have to do much in the way of balancing. The boat accelerated into a turn. Herbie's ears flapped in the wind and he waved his trunk more furiously. It must have been too tight a turn. With a squeal of despair, a mighty crash and an eruption of white water, Herbie lurched over and capsized into the lake. Only the upturned bottoms of the ski floats were to be seen. Somewhere under the surface, still chained to the skis, was Herbie. I struggled through the horrified crowds with the vet attached to the marineland, but by the time we had got round to the point on the lakeside closest to the scene of the accident it was too late. Boats had gone out and found Herbie drowned. Without the chains he would have stood a good chance.

There are other ways of training animals: the results come from the rapport between man and animal and from understanding of animal behaviour rather than from fear and pain. My friends who train dolphins and whales and sealions, Bobby Roberts with his camels, Billy Smart with his elephants, Katja Schumann and her horses, Eddie Wiesinger and his big cats, and hundreds of other trainers of parrots, dogs and kangaroos, get superb results by kindness and communication. Of course there are cruel and abominable methods of training animals just as there are cruel and abominable animal trainers. They are the more despicable because they know that there are better and humane methods that can be and are used. In fact I have found the exponents of fear and torture in animal control to be markedly less successful than those who do it all through a combination of patience, observation, knowledge of animal behaviour and psychology, real affection coupled with respect for the creature, precise oral and visual commands, a consistent attitude, quick and sensitive response to an animal's movements and moods and, most important of all, long training themselves at the hands of good and experienced teachers.

Working in a good circus or marineland where humane methods are practised is immensely enjoyable. In the disreputable few I hope always to be an influence for better standards. Even in a scruffy hell-hole of a travelling menagerie, someone must look after the health of the animals. Moving on from town to town, they receive at best scant attention from a succession of different vets, almost all inexperienced in exotic animal medicine, who rarely have the opportunity to follow through the progress of a case and may well be left with an unpaid bill and a truculent attitude to the next travelling show that passes through. But the bears and monkeys and pumas in these caravans need attention. To spurn them would be to condemn them to even worse miseries, so I try to stimulate improvement of such set-ups from within rather than criticise impotently from without.

From the crucial central point of view, that of the animal, most performing animal acts are in no way detrimental. Some species such as dolphins, sealions, dogs and horses positively revel in their routines, play up to audience applause, benefit from the exercise and go distinctly mopy and morose if laid off for a long time. Of course the elephant awkwardly waltzing on its stand or the chimpanzee that lifts the skirt of its companion and saucily pulls down its knickers are undignified, embarassing and, in some senses, exploited. Elephants are seen at their best charging across the savannahs of Africa, and to watch chimpanzees organizing their lives in the forests is gloriously fascinating. But the embarrassment and shame that we feel is one of guilt in knowing what we are like, what we enjoy, what we have asked them to do. We feel uncomfortable about being part of a human audience that laughs at such outrageous anthropomorphism. The animals are not ashamed and do not have our hang-ups. From their point of view, and that is what matters to me, life is not bad. In a well-run circus nobody hurts them, the bananas are plentiful and at hand, the quarters are snug and warm and they are groomed and cleaned and stroked and fussed over. Many of these animals have been born into the zoo or circus and hand-reared into the business. They are as artificial, as domesticated, as toy poodles or budgerigars or Siamese cats and are far removed from the truly wild members of their species. They have no conception of what life on the outside might be like, they thrive and grow fat and breed and enjoy more freedom in most cases than many lap dogs, pub parrots or flat-bound pussy cats.

Some tricks can only be achieved through cruel methods, to be sure, but they are only a tiny minority and do not figure in the repertoire of a reputable trainer. Provided an animal trusts its trainer and suffers no pain or discomfort, the most complicated 'artificial' behaviour can be achieved. Food, and the greed for it, is the commonest method of persuasion. It is interesting that there seem to be few, if any, occupational diseases of circus animals. I have never heard of a case of waltzing elephant's foot-rot, punch-drunk boxing kangaroos or liberty horse lumbago. Contrast that with the occupational diseases of broiler calves, racing greyhounds, battery hens, sweat-box pigs and hunting horses.

Typically skilled and humane animal trainers are the Naumann family from Germany. They travel all over the world with their big cats and I have spent many hours watching their methods with lions, tigers and pumas. They raise their cats from cubs and work patiently long hours each day, teaching the animals to perform by reward – reward in the form of finger-sized pieces of tender meat, in stroking, patting and praise from familiar voices. No coercion, no pain, no fear. Firmness of course, but that is necessary to train a police horse in its duties or even your own pet dog to fetch the newspaper from the letter box. Do it so, do it right, and see, here is a nice juicy morsel.

By these methods the Naumanns created a unique high-diving tiger act, in which a fully grown Bengal tiger dived into a circular swimming pool from a platform twenty feet above the water. Several years ago the Naumanns arrived with all their gear and their cats for a summer season in the grounds at Belle Vue, Manchester. Work went ahead to assemble the pool, ladder and platform. Everything was set up, but not exactly to order. Somehow the platform was not positioned directly over the centre of the pool as it should have been. This mistake was not apparent to anyone looking from below. Nor, it seems, did the tiger realise anything was wrong when it climbed up the ladder for its first Manchester performance and, after suitable fanfares and drumrolls, launched itself into the air. The flying tiger plunged down into the water but in doing so rapped its back sharply against the metal edge of the pool. In great pain and partially paralysed, the poor animal struggled out of the water and dragged itself to its trainer. The Naumanns were distraught at the pain caused to one of their beloved cats by the carelessness of a member of their team. Within minutes I arrived at the scene to examine the patient.

The collision had produced bleeding and severe tissue damage in the canal carrying the spinal cord down the lower back. The pressure of the blood and swollen soft tissues was pinching the nerve within its bony passageway and as every minute passed the tiger was suffering more pain in the spine and losing the use of its hind legs. The front end of the animal was distinctly aggrieved and in a foul temper. Whatever might be the case with the two hind feet, the front pair and the jaws were in fine fettle. We would have to handle the tiger in its small travelling cage. This was where the kindness and patience of Herr Naumann in training his animals personally since they were tiny cubs paid off.

'Don't worry,' he said to me, opening the little door into the cage. 'You will be able to do whatever you need. I will look after that.'

He squeezed through the opening into the cage and beckoned me to follow. I went in and Herr Naumann's wife closed the door and locked it behind us. There was not much room for the two of us and the tiger. It lay growling and groaning in pain, its tail lying limply, too numb to be switched irritably. Naumann went to the front of the animal and knelt down. Affectionately he took the tiger's head in his hands and brought it onto his lap. He stroked it and talked soothingly in German. The tiger stopped growling and lay impassively.

'Go ahead,' said the trainer, 'He'll be OK now.'

Inwardly I marvelled at his confidence. If there were any fractures waiting for my probing fingers, disturbance of the

43

tortured tissues might well make the animal feel anything but OK. Very gingerly I placed my hands on the muscular back of the big cat, pressing gradually deeper into the tissues, feeling for the spine, tracing the outlines of the vertebrae and running down the sides of the pelvis. The tiger tensed whenever I came across damaged areas and sometimes growled. Naumann tightened his embrace on its head.

The next stage was more delicate. I wanted to feel the inside contours of the pelvis as far as possible, which meant putting two fingers deep inside the anus. I slipped on a finger stall, lubricated my hand and slowly introduced my fingers into the rectum – the first and I suppose the only time that I will ever do that to a conscious adult tiger. The tiger growled and wriggled the front end a bit. He was not amused by this approach, but I was able to satisfy myself that there were no palpable pelvic fractures. It looked as if the lower spine had been badly bruised and jarred. With any luck the soft tissue swelling could be dispelled and the spinal cord would in time return to its normal function. I prepared injections of pain-killers, inflammation-shrinkers and enzymes to speed the removal of damaged cells and blood clots. Naumann continued to murmur away reassuringly while I selected new sharp disposable needles. If there was going to be a sudden nasty reaction it would surely be now as I pricked deep into the muscles. I glanced at Naumann's face, only an inch away from the cat's curved fang teeth. One short-distance blow from the left forefoot would open up his chest like a fork impaling boiled ham. Gritting my teeth, I indicated to Naumann that I was about to strike.

'Go ahead,' he said again. 'He understands we're not here to tease him.'

I stabbed the needle as quickly as I could through the tough skin and deep into the muscle. To my relief the tiger was apparently unaware of the injection and did not stir. Eventually all the drugs were safely inside it. We left the cage and discussed the setting up of an infra-red lamp above the patient's back and the preparation of my favourite invalid food for sick big cats, a sort of steak tartare made of minced steak, raw egg, dried milk powder and sterilised bone flour.

Next day the tiger was much easier but still largely paralysed at the rear, which was causing secondary constipation. It would be necessary to give an enema. I made up a small pail of warm water and soap flakes and primed an ordinary human enema pump. Once again Naumann cradled the head of the tiger in his arms while I filled it up with the soapy solution. Soon I was gratified to be covered in an explosive eruption of froth and tiger excrement, to the apparent relief of the tiger.

Each day the tiger made more and more progress towards recovery. Little by little the power of its hind legs returned although the sluggish bowel action remained for almost two weeks. As the animal became more mobile we had more difficulty in giving the enema. It would rise to its feet with me and my pump still attached to its rectum and, leaving Naumann behind, would spin round in the small cage in an effort to reach the person doing the embarrassing things to its stern. Until Naumann could catch up with the head again and return it firmly to his lap, I had to keep myself, pumping merrily away with one hand and dragging my slopping pail with the other, as close to the animal's bottom as possible. As long as I spun round in the constricted space and did not let the anus get away from me, the cat could not quite reach me with tooth or claw. If the cage had been any larger, constipation might well have triumphed. At last the enemas were over, and a heap of laxative breakfast cereal sliced into the patient's meat for a few days was all that was needed. The tiger made a complete recovery and when I was satisfied that he was a hundred per cent up to scratch I let him go back to the diving board.

Tigers frequently need a little chiropody. Like all cats they try to keep their claws in trim by scratching the earth and, best of all, by dislodging the overgrown outer shell of their nails by raking tree bark. Unfortunately it does not always work and a claw will continue to grow out and round until it digs into the

45

pad of the foot. Then things become unpleasant. The point of the nail produces a painful sore that rapidly becomes infected, and until the nail is cut and the offending portion pulled out of the pad there is no possibility of its healing. It is my job to stop things reaching this stage by regularly looking over the big cats in my care and doing pedicures where necessary. Rather than giving a general anaesthetic for a minor job like this, I try to do it with the animal conscious, by using specially designed restraint cages. At many zoos and safari parks special trapping cages for tigers, lions, leopards and cheetahs have been built with a variety of ingenious devices to immobilise the animals speedily, humanely and conveniently for the veterinary surgeon. Some of these cages have walls that travel in towards one another, controlled by cables and winches from outside. Others have silent descending ceilings like the evil four-posters of Edgar Allan Poe.

One of the most complex systems was built at Manchester by Mr Legge, the former zoo director. A passageway through which the animals pass unconcernedly each day to and from their paddocks conceals a false floor and a roof which can be brought down after the creature has been captured by doors closed in front of and behind it. The roof is a strong mesh of soft rope, stretched within a metal frame, which presses down firmly over the contours of the animal and permits not a flicker of movement. The false floor is removed, revealing a grille of bars on which the underside of the cat is forced to rest. Underneath all this is an inspection pit where I crouch with, of course, an inspection lamp and look up at the belly and feet of my patient. By reaching up I can bring one foot at a time down through the bars, shear off excessive nail and dress any wounds. If necessary I can take a blood sample, give an injection or lance an abscess.

Naturally I found snags in the procedure when I went down to service my first feline. Like the common or garden moggy which finds itself suddenly grabbed and incarcerated out of the blue, the big cat vents its feelings of amazement and

46

apprehension by doing the only things possible in the circumstances, opening its bladder. But between the moggy and the big cat there is one difference in this respect, a difference of enormous degree. Whereas the bladder of your average ginger tom can accommodate a smallish, if noisome, quantity of liquid, the same organ in an adult tiger or lion often holds a pint or two, and somehow the cunning beast contrives always to have it brimming when the chiropodist calls. I was not aware of this prescient control of the feline waterworks when I began working in the newly built cat house in Manchester. I was yet to meet the lion who would wander amiably up to the netting separating him from a small crowd of admiring visitors, turn with his buttocks towards them and expertly spray the front row of the audience with urine. As the dismayed and dampened victims fell about in confusion to the laughter and ridicule of those standing behind, the lion waited patiently in the same position while the dry and unsuspecting guffawers moved forwards into the now vacant stalls. Little did they know that he had, as it were, one barrel still loaded, that all his powder was not spent. When the crowd, now swelled by others who had come running to see what all the fuss was about, was correctly positioned, the cat would look winningly over his shoulder at the clicking cameras and then empty the second half of his bladderful into the throng.

The first time I went down into the cat house inspection pit was for a visit by a photographer from *The Observer* who wanted pictures of a zoo vet for the colour supplement. I would do the chiropody in style, I decided, clad in a surgeon's gown of neat green cotton. The cat was trapped and I slipped down into the narrow sump. Taking up a suitable pose for the photographer who peered down over the edge, I trimmed off a nail or two and held up the bits for the camera. Then it happened. The tiger above opened his water valve to the limit and a cascade of warm yellow liquid poured down onto me and soaked through my gown and underclothes. There was no escaping it. I tried backing off towards the head end. No use. Turning my back simply hastened the soaking of my trousers. Cats have a way of doing these things, as if they have an adjustable nozzle like a rose-spray, and the whole of the air space of the pit was filled with a sort of aerosol effect. I lunged for the metal steps in the wall of the pit and clambered out. Every since then I have made a point of carrying out cat chiropody in oilskins and sou'wester, even though folk in Lancashire used to say that external application of urine was good for the complexion. What would they know about the tiger variety?

Six

Since the principles of good management of performing animals are frequently ignored in the richer, so-called advanced countries, perhaps one should not be surprised that in countries where poverty forces a lower value on human life itself the treatment of exotic animals in captivity would send an appalled shudder through a vet or any animal lover. To dolphins the Far East recently has been like Devil's Island to French convicts: once arrived there they rarely return alive. There has been a lucrative business, largely organised by German theatrical agents, sending pairs of European dolphins out on tours of Thailand, the Philippines, Indonesia, Singapore and Taiwan. Asians adore circuses, travelling shows and novelty exhibitions, particularly where animals are involved. The 'intelligent giant fish', which I believe a majority of the audiences confuse with the feared shark, is immensely popular. The Flipper series of TV shows has been broadcast widely in the Far East and has heightened the interest: every travelling dolphin show naturally has as one of its performers 'the original Flipper direct from Florida, USA'.

The German agents procure the animals in Europe and America and hire them out to Chinese sponsors, who in turn sub-let the shows and sell pieces of the action to syndicates of more Chinese. This is the root of the problem and the key to the numerous disasters that have befallen these hapless creatures. Interested only in the cash return on their investments, totally ignorant of what dolphins are and what they require for good health and condition, often speaking no European language, and ruthless in their commercial dealings, the syndicates have time and again murdered dolphins by incompetence, obduracy and wilful neglect.

Because of the complex network of sub-contracting, the person actually responsible for providing good pool and water conditions and first-class food for the animals is frequently difficult to pin down. Anyway the poor guy with the problem when the animals fall sick or run out of water or find themselves swimming in three feet of thick sewage is the European dolphin trainer. He cannot communicate with the Chinese sponsors direct. His boss has an agreement with the German agent, but both of them are half the world away and in any case the German agent has no more chance of controlling the intricate machinations of an ever-changing group of Chinese businessmen than he has of destroying the Mafia.

So gay little Atlantic bottle-nosed dolphins find themselves in the backyards of Buddhist temples in Singapore's Chinatown, up in the sweating hills of Borneo, or slipped into the bill of a wrestling championship held in a football stadium in downtown Manila. Transport costs are pared down to a minimum: instead of taking a direct jet from Europe to Hong Kong, the animals and trainers find themselves droning along in ancient Dakotas that stop perhaps ten times or more along the route. It is bad enough for the human attendants, who arrive haggard and exhausted after three to four days in the air. But what must the dolphins be experiencing, out of water, unfed and subjected to the din of the engines for half a week?

That is how Andrew and I often come to be flying at a moment's notice to Jakarta or Taipei to try to pick up the pieces of yet another animal tragedy. It may be purely a disease problem or there may be complicating political and economic factors. I have had to wrangle with Chinese entrepreneurs who were trying to save electricity by turning off the big fans that cooled the air in a Singapore stadium. I was not concerned for the audiences, who had to endure the stifling humidity for only three quarters of an hour, but I was anxious about the water temperature of the dolphin pool. It was rising steadily towards the danger point above which the creatures might have difficulty in dispersing their excess body heat. The negotiations were difficult and carried out through an interpreter. It was important not to lose my temper or cause them to lose face. After hours of almost surrealistic exchanges over a matter which to any animal man is painfully, ridiculously obvious, they conceded the point. The fans would be started again.

'What impressed them about you, Dr Taylor,' said the interpreter afterwards, 'was that you are rich and must therefore be someone to be respected as knowing his business.'

'Rich!' I exclaimed. 'Why on earth should they get that idea?' I was hardly well dressed and was sporting no gold teeth or expensive jewellery.

'Your tummy,' replied the interpreter, tapping the results of too much car driving and sitting in aircraft seats. 'You are getting a belly, they said, the sign of the prosperous one.'

The following year I was in Sumatra, dealing with skin disease caused by filthy water when the sponsors had refused to mend a filter pump. A few months later I was called to Bandung in the hill country of Java: a dolphin was seriously ill and there were big problems. I flew out to Jakarta and was met by a representative of the German agents. He had not received the telegram giving my arrival time but had sat on the airport for three days and met every passenger disembarking with 'Dr Taylor, yes?' He whipped me through customs and immigration and took me to a car.

'Only four hours drive to Bandung,' he said.

I was very tired by my long but relatively comfortable jet flight, and wondered what it must have been like for the poor dolphins. After being unloaded from the aircraft they too must have set off by road, but in a wagon taking far longer than four hours over the bumpy roads into the high country.

I am not sure what my companion was thinking nor to which branch of the show-biz fraternity I belonged when he said: 'Before we go any further, Doctor, I should warn you that all

51

artistes who have come to Java up to this time, without exception, have caught VD.'

'Oh, thank you very much,' I murmured.

We passed over a wooden bridge spanning a shallow wooded valley. Below in the stream a young woman with long gleaming black hair and a green and red batik sarong paddled naked from the waist upwards. It was a warm, scented evening with a sky of fluorescent salmon pink. We bounced along, climbing steadily through hills neatly stepped with paddy fields and crusted with dense green tea plantations. We slipped over the range and dropped down into Bandung, a bustling, friendly city, full of colour and the babble of voices, of old Dutch colonial villas, neat little houses covered with lush tropical vegetation, higgledy-piggledy conglomerations of shanties, temples, and colourful bird markets, swarms of rickshaws and charming, beautiful people. I went straight to the dolphin pool, in one of the poorer quarters. A simple pair of portable plastic swimming pools stood in the middle of an arena made from wooden laths and partly roofed with palm leaves. The water was brown and contained a high concentration of particles: it looked for all the world like oxtail soup but smelled like rotten fish. Juan the dolphin trainer, an old friend from England, was in a terrible state over his animals. One was very ill and losing weight by the hour, and to cap it all the Chinese sponsors had cut up rough. Sick dolphin, they had said, meant no show. No show meant no people. No people meant they were not going to pay money for electricity or water or salt or food. Two people had been killed the day before in the crush trying to get into the arena to see Flipper. Now the police were on guard outside.

In my usual tropical kit, my underpants, I jumped into the pool to examine the sick dolphin, Rocky. He was in a bad way, with thin, diseased skin and half-closed, lethargic eyes. I went over him carefully and found an enlarged liver lobe bulging back beyond the last rib which suggested liver disease. When working in the East I rarely have problems getting blood samples processed, since there is usually a mission hospital or similar institution with a lab only too willing to help out in an emergency. Sure enough, within half an hour I had located an American Pentecostal hospital who readily agreed to analyse a blood sample from Rocky. A couple of hours later the results came back. It was hepatitis. The dolphin was in danger of complete liver collapse and death within a very short space of time. I went back to the pool and opened the bag of tricks that I always carry with me. I had little doubt that the infection had come from the foul water, though the fish that were being fed to the dolphins looked none too wholesome either. It would take a few days to identify exactly the bacterium responsible, and by then Rocky might be dead. I decided to assume that the germ causing the liver infection was one of a group which often affects dolphins: a frequenter of water and bad fish, it is totally resistant to penicillin and most antibiotics. I would have to use a drug rarely employed as yet in treating animals in Britain, the highly efficient gentamycin. Years before at Flamingo Park in Yorkshire I had experimented and found that because dolphin kidneys are more efficient at throwing the stuff out, three times the dose for an equivalent weight of human being was needed to achieve a curative level of gentamycin in the dolphin blood-stream. At this rate it would cost around sixty pounds a day for Rocky's antibiotic alone, without the drugs to aid the weakening liver cells and replace chemicals that the organ was too weak to manufacture. Also, it is no good giving gentamycin by mouth as it just is not absorbed from the bowel. Rocky would need to be injected four times a day.

So began an intensive course of treatment to clear the dolphin's system of the poisons building up because of the liver failure. He was unable to take part in any performances and Flipper his mate was unwilling to do any tricks without him. The management were up in arms about it; it was most uncooperative and inconsiderate of the animal to fall ill. What about the paying customers, who would give their right arms to get in? And why, now that the dolphin doctor from England had given the animal the once-over and an injection of golden liquid, wasn't the wretched Rocky hard at it again? Hadn't he heard? The show must go on!

A compromise of sorts had to be reached. I was adamant that Rocky would rest like the serious hospital case he was; they wanted rupiahs from the punters. So it came about that the public were admitted four times a day to watch an extraordinary kind of dolphin show. When all the customers were packed into the rows of seats around the pool, the compère would do his usual warm-up introduction to the amazing 'lumba-lumbas' as the dolphins are called in Indonesian. He would explain that Rocky was a bit off colour so Flipper would not do his stuff very well, but, he would add, he had a special treat for the crowd. At great expense, all the way from England, the management had brought that unique, that amazing, that incredible per-forming dolphin doctor! Applause from the audience. For the first time ever in Asia, complete with hypodermic needle, stethoscope but no baggy trousers, Dr David Taylor will examine and inject the sick Rocky! At this point ninety-five per cent of the audience stand on their seats for a better view. And now to introduce the man who knows all the secrets of a lumba-lumba's sex life! The tape-recording of 'A Life on the Ocean Wave' is turned up to maximum volume. Your friend and mine, Dr Taylor from Lancashire, England!

Out from the fish-kitchen I walk. The audience grin, cheer and applaud enthusiastically. With a great show of net-twirling Juan and his assistants catch the torpid dolphin. I bow to the crowd, wave my stethoscope in the air, then get down to the serious business of giving Rocky his essential treatment. When it comes to the filling of the syringe with the gentamycin I hold up the bottles so that the audience can see every detail of the process. The empty vials are eagerly sought after by small boys in the front row. There is a great a-a-a-ah from the crowd as I insert the needle and more clapping as I withdraw it and rub the site with an antiseptic swab.

54

Four times a day, *pace* Equity and the Royal College of Veterinary Surgeons, I trod the boards, and by the end of the week Rocky was coming back strongly and the sponsors had coined a small fortune. The trouble was that the fortune was not big enough, nowhere near what they had hoped for. A few days after I began my act I had bigger trouble than ever. The leader of the syndicate came to the arena one evening and personally removed all the fuses, venting his anger with the German agent on the innocent dolphins. Now they were totally unfiltered. Without an amp of electricity in the place there were no lights for my night injections and the fish in the refrigerator were rapidly going bad. I was livid. The sponsor had gone into a deep huff and refused to see Juan or the representative of the German agent. Flipper and Rocky cruised around in even thicker oxtail soup. I put a ban on feeding the putrefying fish and went to see the Chinese sponsor. Whether he liked it or not, I would sit on his doorstep until I had words with him. Eventually I was let in and invited to talk with him.

'I bear you personally no ill will,' he said, 'but these animals that cannot work are causing me much anguish. It is not just money, it is a political problem. You see, we Chinese in countries like Indonesia have to be very careful. There are racial tensions here although you may not sense it at the moment. Last year a Chinese sponsor promoted a show here in Bandung and something went wrong, he didn't give the people what he'd promised, and it sparked off an explosion of resentment among the native Indonesian majority. They took it out on all the Chinese community, not just the sponsor. Cars of Chinese had their windscreens broken and tyres slashed. Some houses were set on fire. It could easily happen again. Chinese businessmen in the Far East are widely resented by other races in the community. I really believe we Chinese sit on a tinder box. So if the dolphin show that I promote this year is regarded as a wash-out and doesn't come up to the Indonesians' expectations, I could have big trouble. And so could all the other Chinese in Bandung. That is why we don't use banks for our savings but hoard little gold ingots. You can never tell what will happen tomorrow.'

So it was yet another political affair involving dolphins.

'But you must see my point of view also,' I replied. 'I am here solely to look after the health of the dolphins. The sooner Rocky is OK, the sooner the show can be a big hit.'

The Chinaman nodded impassively but returned to his theme of racial tension. 'Three days ago two people were killed, you know, trying to get into the show. How many next time? And suppose they blame it on me? I'd be crucified.'

On and on we wrangled but I made no headway. He was not going to spend money on keeping the dolphins unless they worked. In desperation I tried a different tack.

'Right then,' I said, standing up to go, 'as you can do nothing for the animals, I myself personally must pay for the replacement of the fuses and the water and electricity bills. The animals are not my property. I have no interest in the show. I am not an employee of the German agent nor a shareholder in your syndicate. But we British are at least humane and civilised enough to protect the weak and innocent' (I hoped he had not heard of our fine English stag- and otter-hunters and the hare-coursing fraternity) 'and, though I cannot afford it, I cannot see the dolphins die. Good evening.'

I walked smartly towards the door. Can't the bastard lose some of this notorious Oriental face, I thought. Perhaps it doesn't exist. As I reached the door, to my astounded delight he called me back.

'Dr Taylor,' he said, 'I have no quarrel with you. I will make enquiries to see who removed the fuses. The electricity will be on within the hour.'

Good Lord, I thought, it really has worked. I've shamed him, and to avoid losing face he's suggesting that someone else turned off the power. Still, I had no wish to embarrass him and did not let on that I knew who had pulled the fuses.

'How very good of you!' I said, shaking his hand heartily. 'I'll do my best to have Rocky in A1 shape as soon as possible.' To improve things further I offered to mediate between him and the German agents and to thrash out a more reasonable arrangement for the rest of the tour.

Rocky recovered splendidly and eventually he and Flipper came back to Europe for a well-earned rest. But they brought something else back with them. From some batch of contaminated fish or pool of unwholesome water in Asia they had picked up a virus. This evil little germ lay dormant in their bodies for many weeks but in time it became active and began to multiply rapidly within the cells of the dolphins. Intensive efforts were made to destroy the germ, which like all viruses was resistant to antibiotics, but after a long period of illness both Rocky and Flipper died.

No-one ever really escaped from Devil's Island.

Seven

When the whale trainer walked into the dolphinarium at Flamingo Park early one morning he could not believe his eyes. The deep, hour-glass-shaped pool in which the killer whale, Cuddles, had lived for three years was no longer brimming with clear blue artificial sea water. Instead the entire pool was filled with murky scarlet liquid. He felt a sickening contraction of his stomach. Something terrible had happened to the whale. Surely the sixteen-foot-long animal must be lying disembowelled on the bottom of the pool. But no – with the usual blast of steaming breath, Cuddles' shining black head suddenly emerged from the red soup. He was alive. The trainer dashed down to the basement and peered through the underwater windows. It was like looking into a crimson fog, a pea-souper with less than six inches visibility.

It was only a few days after my return from Java and my theatrical debut with Rocky and Flipper, but when I received the frantic telephone call I set off for the zoo immediately. Obviously, I thought, someone is exaggerating rather in the heat of the moment. Whales bleed like any other animal when injured, but to turn 250,000 gallons completely red? Impossible! OK, whales are big creatures and Cuddles weighed over two and a half tons, but how much blood did they think such an animal could carry in his circulation system? Horror erased such thoughts the instant I saw the pool. It was actually true. The water looked like somewhat anaemic blood. We all know that blood stains easily and that a little goes a long way: every veterinary surgeon has been called to see a dog with a cut foot where the scene of the accident or the house in which it is being attended looks as if a dozen pigs had been slaughtered there. But this was something unbelievable.

Cuddles floated quietly in the middle of the pool. His deep black body colour had taken on more of a dark grey shade. When I called him over to the side he responded slowly. This was not the perky, mischievous creature that I knew so well, who would call to me with his high-pitched piggy squeal whenever I passed through the crowd of spectators. He was torpid and depressed. His gums and the membrane round his eye, normally a deep pink colour, were now a death-like white. I enquired about his appetite. Zero. For the first time since he had arrived in Yorkshire, Cuddles' enormous appetite for herring and mackerel had vanished. He would not face even a single fish.

I was highly alarmed. Of all the animals with which I have worked I have been closer to none than to Cuddles. Despite the species' fearsome-sounding name, and although in the wild state they are voracious and deadly hunters, killer whales in captivity are generally amenable and gentle to the humans who look after them. I had been with Cuddles when he arrived one frosty winter night, a plump and genial baby with teeth just cutting through his gums. Through the summers we had played daily together in the water. He loved to hug you with his flippers while he floated vertically and you tickled his smooth round belly with your toes. Tug-of-war with an old car tyre, carrying a rider round on his back either in front of his dorsal fin or behind, on what I called the rumble seat where the ride was bumpy and exhilarating; he had played eagerly all day. As a patient he had been impeccable. Martin Padley, his trainer, and I had designed a special examination sling that ran out over Cuddles' pool on telescopic girders. Not only was he easy to get into it for routine blood sampling or vaccination but he was positively reluctant to leave this aquatic examination couch! Martin always had to entice him out rather than in. There had been the awful time when he swallowed a child's plastic trumpet and submitted placidly to stomach pumping,

59

and he had been highly co-operative as a donor in a unique attempt at long-distance artificial insemination of another whale in Cleethorpes. I had learnt most of my techniques of whale handling and medication on this fellow. Now it seemed that I was about to lose him through some systerious calamity.

The first priority was to find out where the blood was coming from. There was no sign of a wound on his upper surface as he bobbed in the water. I put on a wet-suit and jumped into the pool. The crimson water smelt dank and unpleasant. I paddled across to my friend and hugged his head. Cuddles gazed at me with his round dark eyes but made no move to cuddle up to me as he usually did. Ominously, the healthy syrupy tears no longer flowed from his eyelids. Cuddles was dehydrating somehow, bleeding to death.

I went all over his back and tail flukes: so sign of any injury. Then, using his paddle-like left flipper as a lever, I laboriously rolled him over in the water. His gleaming white abdomen broke the water surface. Not a trace of a wound could I see. There were now only two possibilities: the blood was coming out either with his urine or in his stools. Suddenly, as he floated like a great capsized plastic boat, a massive welter of what seemed to be almost pure blood gushed out of his anus. That was it. Cuddles was bleeding massively somewhere in his intestines.

Climbing out of the pool, I gave instructions for it to be emptied immediately. Whatever the problem was, it had struck rapidly out of the blue. Cuddles had been normal up to the previous evening when all the dolphinarium staff went home. It seemed to be affecting the lower bowel: if the bleeding source was in the stomach or high in the bowel the blood would have been partly digested and changed to a much darker brown or black colour on its way through the intestinal tract. I suspected bacterial or virus infection producing rapid ulceration of the bowel lining. If it was a bacterium, perhaps the culprit was the evil salmonella, a food poisoning germ which causes diarrhoea and the passing of blood in other animals

60

Whatever the cause, my first priority now was to get Cuddles down onto the dry bottom of the pool, examine him thoroughly and take blood samples to see how bad the damage was. Next I had to stop the bleeding and replace some of the liquid that his circulation had lost. When the volume of circulating blood becomes too small to carry enough oxygen and other vital supplies to key organs, shock and death speedily set in. How to expand Cuddles' blood volume? I decided that in any event I had to make preparations for some sort of transfusion. Ideally I wanted many pints of killer whale blood, not quite the sort of stuff that is usually available at the local blood bank! We knew that there were certainly three major blood groups in bottle-nosed dolphins, but no-one knew anything about the blood groups of whales. The nearest captive killers were in America. Perhaps some of my colleagues out there had some suitable blood stored.

I telephoned all the major marinelands in the United States and explained my predicament. No-one had any killer whale blood stored and no-one had come across a similar problem. My friend Dr White at Miami Seaquarium had had a case of severe bleeding in a whale that had crashed through an underwater viewing window. It had needed lots of surgery and supportive medical therapy but no blood transfusions had been given. Would anyone fancy volunteering one of their whales as a donor of a dozen or two pints? I could easily get the stuff shipped over express on the next Pan-Am or TWA flight. The answer was always the same. Highly valuable animals. The difficulty of having to drain pools in the middle of the show season in order to take blood. Anyway, how were we to be sure without wasting days testing samples whether any particular whale's blood would be compatible with Cuddles'? Whole blood transfusion was out.

The fire brigade arrived. Whenever we needed to speed up the emptying of the pools they were called in. Half an hour later, an unusually dark grey and very white whale was lying passively on the concrete bottom of the pool while hoses and buckets were used to keep his skin moist. I went down and took blood from the big blood vessel in his tail. Even to the naked eye the sample appeared watery and thin. The crucial analyses were quickly done in the laboratory at the pool side. As I had feared, Cuddles had lost a great deal of blood into the intestines. Normally he carried a regular seventeen grammes of haemoglobin, the red oxygen-carrying constituent, in every hundred c.c.'s of his blood. Now it was down to only ten grammes. The total number of red blood cells had also dropped precipitously. Other tests showed no sign of active bacterial infection or liver or kidney damage.

A trainer came into the laboratory carrying what looked like a fragment of wet white paper. 'He's just passed another load of blood,' he reported, 'and there was this in it.'

The specimen was sticky and fragile. I dropped it into a beaker of cold water and teased it out with a needle. It unfolded into a delicate white film as big as a postage stamp. The film was not completely intact for at three or four points there were round holes ringed distinctly by reddish-brown material. It was a piece of intestinal lining membrane and the holes were ulcers surrounded by blood pigment, a valuable find but a depressing one. Cuddles had actively bleeding multiple ulcers in his bowels. If there were so many on this small fragment, how many thousands more might there be if the entire hundred feet of his intestines were similarly involved?

The bit of bowel lining and some swabs went to the bacteriology laboratory for urgent examination and I then returned to the problem of replacing Cuddles' lost blood volume. I had to take second best. Although it had no oxygen-carrying power, transfusions of artificial plasma would combat many of the shock-producing factors and would stop the blood vessels from literally collapsing. It was going to mean putting Cuddles on an intravenous drip, and I estimated that at least forty pints would be required. An urgent call for help was sent out to Leeds General Hospital. They readily agreed to upply us with a hundred bottles of the life-saving liquid and it was despatched by fast car under police escort. Meanwhile I filled Cuddles with other important drugs to tackle the sadly abused bowels. Through the giant one-foot-long needle I injected things like vitamins, anti-inflammatory drugs and antibiotics. Although it would take ten to fourteen days for it to be assembled into the essential haemoglobin, I gave big shots of iron liquid. He would need the iron reserves if he recovered.

When the cases of artificial plasma arrived I started work on the transfusion. I used a special needle-like tube of the sort we had employed when doing electrocardiographic investigations on Cuddles some weeks before. The tube had to be inserted accurately into a tail vein. In both dolphins and killer whales, veins and arteries near the surface are closely intermingled for heat-exchange purposes, and if any of the liquid from an intravenous injection goes into an artery there can be nasty repercussions including profound sloughing and death of a large area of tail skin. Kneeling with Cuddles' great tail held above my head I inserted the tube and checked and double-checked that the blood oozing from it was coming only from a vein. When I was satisfied that all was well I connected the plastic tubes to the plasma bottle and adjusted the dosage regulator. A keeper stood on a chair holding the bottle high in the air so that the flow of liquid was not counteracted by Cuddles' massive heart pressure.

Slowly the golden fluid seeped into the whale's system. After ten minutes I switched to the second bottle. Although whale blood does not clot easily, I had anticipated trouble with the tube in the vein and had used a chemical to inhibit clotting and consequent blockage, but I felt sure that frequent changes of the tube would be necessary. In fact, as the hours passed slowly by, the keepers holding the bottles and the bottles themselves were the only things to be changed. The tube remained unblocked throughout the whole ten hours of the transfusion. Cuddles was as good as gold. Not once did he protest or wriggle.

The man holding the tail up during all this time refused to be relieved. He, too, was deeply involved with the animal and wanted to do everything in his power to help. It was cold and damp in the pool bottom so I sent for a bottle of rum to ward off inner chills. From time to time I insisted on the tail holder taking a good pull from the rum bottle. So solicitous was I for the man's health that I did not realise how many tots he had taken during the long hours of waiting. When it was all finished we discovered the good man to be totally drunk and incapable and had to hoist him out of the pool in a dolphin sling.

We refilled the pool. To my delight, when it was up to the six-foot mark Cuddles accepted a few fish. It was terrible to see the chalk-white back of his throat when he opened his jaws to take them but at least the boy was eating again! I stopped the refilling at eight feet. It was good to see clear blue water again but what if he continued to bleed?

Next morning I held my breath as I went into the dolphinarium. My heart sank like an express lift when I saw the glum expressions on the faces of the trainers. The pool water was deep scarlet again. We drained immediately and once more took a blood sample. The haemoglobin and red cell counts were lower than before, below the point at which, in humans, a blood transfusion becomes imperative. I transfused the plasma again, gave more injections and passed a stomach tube. Cuddles took it all philosophically. Through the stomach tube I pumped in a peculiar pink mixture which I had concocted in a large unused plastic dustbin. It contained water and honey, mineral salts to replace those lost in the bleeding, glucose, rose-hip syrup, invalid food, kaolin to soothe the inflamed bowel, and Guinness. As it by-passed his taste buds I do not suppose Cuddles relished it or otherwise. The next day things looked much brighter – Cuddles had not bled overnight and showed an improved appetite. The following day dawn broke for the third time on a scene of gory water, but analysis showed the blood loss to have been much reduced and the haemoglo

64

in level, though still below the critical minimum, was levelling out. Still seriously worried, but no longer in complete despair, repeated my injections and the dustbin mixture.

By now the laboratory results were all back. No bacteria were involved. The cause of the ulcers remained a mystery, as it does to this day, although I strongly believe a virus to have been the culprit. Cuddles continued to eat quite well and even agreed to play gently. He did not haemorrhage on the day after the third bleeding, nor on the next day or the one after that. I became increasingly hopeful. The whale was still very pale but steadily growing stronger and I fortified his fish by packing them with hunks of cooked Lancashire black puddings, rare delicacies made from blood and fat.

Cuddles never bled again. His recovery was fast and free from further incident. Two weeks after the first attack his blood analysis was halfway back to normal and in a further three weeks it was completely satisfactory. By this time he was greedily gulping down whole undisguised black puddings by the dozen and opening his now salmon-pink mouth with alacrity to have foaming quarts of Guinness poured straight into his gullet.

Many things about Cuddles' bleeding disease I do not understand, and which if any of my lines of treatment helped to save the day will never be known. Certainly the transfusions only averted death from shock and tackled some of the circulatory complications. Perhaps it was the kaolin or the anti-inflammatory drugs or the black puddings that turned the tide against the ulcers. Perhaps if a virus was involved Cuddles developed a rapid immunity which effectively combated the attack. A Devonshire woman working at Flamingo Park as personal secretary to the director had a different view on the affair. When it was all over we were talking and she told me what she had done to help the dying killer whale.

'When he bled the third time I went and phoned a wise woman in my home village in the West Country,' she told me. 'She's a person who uses white magic on warts and styes and

65

rheumatism. Marvellous reputation. Never known to fail.

'What did you say to her?' I asked.

'I told her briefly what was wrong at the dolphinarium and she just said that everything would be all right, and that the bleeding would stop when I put the receiver down.'

It sounded like the most ridiculous humbug to me, but I respected the director's secretary as an astute and intelligent woman.

'Well,' I said, 'can you remember the time when you finished speaking to your wise woman acquaintance?'

'Of course I can,' she replied with an odd smile. 'It was eight-thirty in the morning.'

I walked down to the dolphinarium and looked in the record book. Every minute item concerning the whale and dolphins in health and sickness is logged there day by day, year in and year out. On the morning of the third and final episode of Cuddles' bleeding a trainer had recorded the last occasion on which the whale was seen to pass blood. The time was entered as 8.31 a.m.

Eight

Although the fascination of tending exotic animals is endless, it is not every day that a vet is faced with a life and death emergency like the drama of Cuddles' bleeding. All the same, what may start as a comparatively simple task (if such a thing may be said to exist in a zoo vet's work) can develop into a situation calling for rapid action if a valuable animal is to be saved. For example, a new hippopotamus, Hercules, arrived one afternoon at the zoo in Manchester. He had been sent from Whipsnade in a massive crate made out of thick wooden beams reinforced with steel bands. The hippo is not a creature to be trifled with. He can hurl himself forwards or spin round on his hind feet with remarkable agility, he is as unstoppable as a tank and he delivers a fearsome chomping, crushing bite. To be on the safe side, Whipsnade had given Hercules a dose of phencyclidine before sending him off and had strongly recommended that he should receive a further shot just before he was uncrated in Manchester. They feared that otherwise, once the door of the crate was opened, a highly irascible hippo might emerge and make his way like an express train, walls and so on notwithstanding, towards the city centre.

Hercules' crate was open-topped and by climbing up the side I could look down on the steaming armour-plating of the big hippopotamus. He was standing calmly enough without any sign of agitation and showing little sign of the effects of the sedative. I had not unloaded a hippo before. My inclination would have been to forgo the second phencyclidine injection but Whipsnade, with much more experience of these matters at the time, had made the point strongly. They had even sent a

67

measured dose of the drug. I filled a syringe, bent down over the side of the crate and slapped my stoutest needle through the hippo's rump. Hercules reacted by slamming my wrist hard against the wooden side of the crate. I was trapped securely. Hercules maintained the pressure against my wrist with all his might. He wiggled his hips a bit and ground my hand excruciatingly into the wood. Biting my tongue, I slapped vainly at the hippo's bottom with my other hand. It was some minutes before he conceded to pull away and I could retrieve my extremity, now numb, black and horribly scuffed. Twenty years later I still have no feeling in that part of my wrist.

After a quarter of an hour Hercules was still standing but his ears were drooping slightly and there was a string of saliva hanging from his jaw. I decided to let him out. The bolts were removed from the reinforced door and the door was opened wide. We were using the rear door to make him back out so that he would be less likely to charge. Hercules did not budge. No matter what we did, tapping his nose with a stick, tempting him with food or slapping his back, he was not inclined to go into reverse gear. So we cautiously opened the front door, revealing fully the bucolic features of Hercules for the first time. He stared blandly at the inside of the tropical river house where he was now to live, sniffed disdainfully and blinked his drowsy eyelids. Then he saw the shining pool of warm water for him, its surface wreathed in misty vapour. Very sedately Hercules began to move forwards. He emerged from the crate, paused briefly, then walked slowly towards the pool. He went down the ramp at the side of the pool as if on tiptoe, sniffed at the water, found it to his liking and very gracefully slipped in. Through the clear water, not yet sullied by hippo droppings, we could see him settle peacefully on the bottom of the pool and then, gradually it seemed, fall asleep. The second dose of phencyclidine, together with the soothing warm bath, was having an understandable but potentially lethal effect. A conscious hippo can hold its breath underwater for many minutes but will

68

eventually come to the surface to take in a fresh gulp of air. A doped hippo might very well be a different matter. Suppose Hercules inhaled blissfully while dreaming on the bottom of his pool? A cluster of icicles formed in the pit of my stomach.

'It looks as if he's going to sleep,' I told the keepers around me. 'Get some ropes – fast. We could be in big trouble!'

Some of the men dashed off. The zoo director and I stood at the water's edge looking anxiously down at the recumbent form of the hippo three feet below the surface. When the ropes arrived there was only one thing for it. Stripping off to our underpants, Matt Kelly and I jumped into the water and dived for the submerged hulk. It is no easy task to feel one's way over a hippo's anatomy without the benefit of a pair of goggles and towing a length of thick rope. Spluttering we both surfaced for a quick discussion on a plan of action.

'You try to get a rope on the back legs, Matt,' I said. 'I'll see if I can get one round the neck.'

Matt dived again and I followed. Hercules slumbered on, unaware of the visitors struggling clumsily about his submarine bedroom. I would not dare to take such liberties with a hippo in full possession of its senses. After much effort and repeated returns to the surface with bursting lungs we managed to place the ropes more or less as we wanted them. The keepers hauled on the ropes and to my relief Hercules, most un-Venus-like, rose to the surface. The great nostrils opened as his head cleared the water and he exhaled gently. His eyes were half closed and there was a pleasant softening of the hippo's usual grim smile.

It was impossible to drag the heavy creature onto land. There were not enough of us, hippos have no convenient handles, and I was afraid that the excessive use of ropes on Hercules' limbs and neck might injure him. In water he weighed much less, so we would have to support him in the pool by passing ropes under his belly until he was no longer under the influence. We kept the crucial head up by wrapping towels round it and slinging it to a beam. Hercules looked for all the

69

world as if he was suffering an attack of toothache and had taken to the whisky bottle to alleviate the pain.

After some hours Hercules began to wriggle on the supporting ropes. His eyes opened fully and he surveyed the strange scene sombrely. When he realised that his towel bandage inhibited chomping he became restless and we decided that he had come round enough to look after himself. After being untangled he retired to the bottom of the pool from which secure position he looked up at us lugubriously. Several minutes later I watched him come to the surface to breathe deeply. Hercules was going to be all right.

Hercules was indeed all right. He immediately fell in love with his pool set in an imitation tropical jungle with waterfalls, islands and luscious vegetation. His arrival, however, spelt disaster for some other denizens of the Manchester jungle. Sharing his habitat were tapirs, capybaras and an assortment of exotic birds. These Hercules proceeded to stalk and, if possible, eat. He would play the crocodile, lurking beneath the surface of the water now dark with his droppings, and using his protuberant eyes as mini-periscopes. When a tapir came down to drink or a bird perched on a rock at the water's edge, Hercules would glide stealthily in like a killer submarine. With a sudden charge when he was within inches of his prey he would seize it in his jaws and kill it instantly with one powerful crunch. Then Hercules the hippo would feast until not a scrap remained. So much for vegetarianism: Hercules fancied meat and he still does. Sometimes when he is off colour I stand on the rocks by his pool and toss him loaves packed with pick-me-ups or stimulants. I have to watch carefully for the pair of gleaming eyes that just about break the water surface and come slowly but steadily towards my feet. At such moments I skip smartly backwards.

Hercules would seem to relish a taste of vet's meat to break the monotony of his orthodox diet, and perhaps it is for the same reason that zoo animals so often swallow unusual objects. Sometimes these things are ingested accidentally but at other times there may be special reasons for them being taken in voluntarily, as in the case of the sealion, which in the wild can often be found carrying a few stones quite harmlessly in its stomach. These stones act as ballast to help the animal dive, rather like the weighted belt of a skin diver: thus deeper diving species of sealion tend to carry more ballast than the shallower diving species. In captivity this natural, fairly limited taking on of stones can go wrong. Where sealions are kept in fresh water with no access to salt, particularly if the pool is a simple one scooped out of the earth, the animal may attempt to satisfy its craving for salt in its diet by eating soil and stones. To avoid this I try to see that all the sealions and seals in my care that are not in saltwater pools have table salt added daily to their fish diet.

Unfortunately, I still see the results of stone-swallowing by sealions over a long period, as when a sealion at a safari park in England died suddenly after a lengthy spell of erratic eating. For months it had been keen to feed but quickly lost its appetite after being given one or two fish. Then, as if it had just had a Chinese meal, it would be hungry and calling for fish within half an hour. The owners had not worried unduly because the sealion seemed to be actually gaining weight. Indeed it was! When I looked at the body it had a plump rounded belly that must surely be full of fat. I began the autopsy and within seconds of slicing through the abdominal wall was faced with an amazing sight. The sealion was, in fact, skinny and free of healthy fat stores. The stomach, which is normally about the same size and shape as a human's and lies tucked neatly away under the rib cage, was horribly distended. It filled the abdomen, squeezing the liver and kidneys and intestines. It bulged everywhere, particularly back towards the tail. I could not see the end of it; it continued on into the pelvic cavity where only the bladder and associated organs should be found. Inside the stomach were stones, hundreds and hundreds of them packing every bit of available space and stretching the stomach wall until it was as thin as tissue paper. When they were all removed they filled three gallon buckets

71

and weighed almost forty pounds. It was the worst foreign
body load I had ever seen.

There were other sealions in the safari park of the same age
as the poor dead individual. What about them? They were
fit-looking animals who delighted in performing their skilful
feats of balance before the visitors. All looked well, but I was of
a mind to X-ray the lot of them to make certain that no more
were carrying around stomachs like gravel pits. I asked the
trainer whether there were any abnormal symptoms to report.
He thought for a moment and began to shake his head.

'No, I don't think so except . . .' He frowned and then
carried on. 'Except for Mimi. She's a little bit like Otto, the
dead one, always hungry but very easily filled.'

I walked over to where Mimi stood elegantly on her show
stand. She sniffed diffidently at me and clapped her front
flippers hopefully. I could see no sign of trouble brewing.
Then the trainer called Mimi off the stand and she slipped
down onto the ground and hauled herself towards the fish
bucket. As she passed I heard a soft and unusual sound, like
the lapping of water on a shingle beach, the rush of pebbles
one upon another. There was too much incidental noise from
the other animals and the visitors to hear it clearly so I had
Mimi taken to the quiet of the hospital. There I listened again.
When she moved it was possible to hear the crunching,
grinding noise of gravel. I stroked her and made friends and
then carefully pressed her stomach. Scr-r-runch. It was exactly
like digging into a bag of marbles. Mimi was full of rocks.

Although, along with the giraffe, the sealion is one of the
more difficult animals to anaesthetise (its ability to hold its
breath as if diving can cause problems with anaesthetic gas
machines), I decided to operate. Opening the stomach of a dog
to remove swallowed objects is a common and not very diffcult
operation but the sealion is somewhat trickier. A particular risk
is post-operative infection from the skin, which literally teems
with all sorts of nasty bacteria. For the surgeon, too, contact
with sealion skin and other tissues can be risky if there are any

cuts in his rubber gloves and abrasions on his hands. A germ often found living harmlessly on sealion skin can attack pigs, dolphins and other animals dramatically, and in humans may set up the unpleasant infection known as 'blubber finger' or 'seal hand' to generations of seal skinners and whaling men.

From Mimi's stomach one by one I retrieved 124 stones weighing almost sixteen pounds altogether. No wonder she had been hungry, with nowhere to accommodate a decent meal. When she was stitched up Mimi was a much more streamlined creature. I looked forward to seeing her eat a hearty meal of three or four pounds of herring in a few days after the stomach sutures had done their work and she could come off the post-operative diet of liquidised fish and water.

Other animals have eaten odd things as well. The elephant at Belle Vue Zoo that took an umbrella did not seem to suffer the slightest twinge of the collywobbles, although an enormous old elephant seal at Cleethorpes found a woolly cardigan too much for it and tragically choked to death. It is not always necessary to approach the stomach by operation through the abdomen, since increasingly nowadays, particularly in dolphins, the arch-swallowers of bric-à-brac, we employ an ingenious piece of equipment normally used for exploring the higher reaches of the human bowel. This is the Olympus fibre-optic gastro-scope, a very expensive device which can do wonders when slipped simply and without anaesthetic down the animal's throat. It is thin and flexible and carries a powerful light source, a mobile viewing tip, a water spray, an air tube for inflating organs to be inspected, and a host of special attach-ments. Looking through the eyepiece we can see magnified and in full colour every nook and cranny in the stomach and even further down into the intestine or up the bile duct. The tip can be made to go round corners and to look backwards towards the viewer. By passing minute instruments down within the tube we can cauterise bleeding points, take biopsy samples of diseased tissue and grab or lasso objects. The stomach and bowels expanded by air from the gastroscope

73

become fascinating caverns and grottoes through which by remote control we can wander in search of the bizarre and the diseased.

It was by using this machine that we took the first colour photographs ever made of the inside of a living dolphin. Since then we have begun to build up a reference library of slides of the various bacterial, fungal and other ailments that can attack the crucial three stomachs of our cetacean friends. One of the first patients on which we used the fibre-optic gastroscope was Brandy, a talented star of the dolphin show at Marineland in Palma Nova, Majorca. One day, for no apparent reason, Brandy swallowed one of the soft plastic rings, six inches across, which he played with during his performances. Down into his stomach it went and down it stayed. Nothing untoward happened at first, and Brandy continued to eat and work normally. But the powerful acids in his stomach were slowly vulcanising the plastic and turning the soft ring into something much more hard and irritant. David Mudge, the director of Marineland and an old friend in the dolphin business, became worried when the ring was not regurgitated as he had hoped. What was more, after some days Brandy began to look unwell. He became irritable, his work became erratic and his appetite disappeared. David was certain that Brandy was experiencing stomach pain.

We had talked together over the telephone when the ring was first swallowed and had decided to observe the animal and to treat him conservatively at first. Now it became obvious that we would have to intervene with strong positive measures. Andrew, my partner, flew out to Majorca with the fibre-optic gastroscope and accompanied by David Wild, the most skilled 'driver', as he calls himself, of the complex instrument in the country. Brandy certainly looked ill. He was pale, seemed tense and in pain, and his usual cheeky, vivacious temperament had changed to one of irritable misery. No longer was he cock of the male dolphins in Palma Nova, forever paying court to his harem of admiring females. Blood analysis showed

74

strong evidence of bleeding ulcers in his stomach. Without further ado Brandy was caught, hauled out of the pool and placed on a soft rubber mattress.

Dolphins out of water produce a lot of body heat and unless they are kept wet may overheat and show dangerous cracking and peeling of the skin. A man stood by with a bucket wetting the animal down while Andrew completed his preparations. First, wet towels were wrapped round Brandy's upper and lower jaws and used to pull the mouth open and hold it open. Gently, Andrew passed the lubricated gastroscope over the back of the dolphin's tongue, to one side of the larynx and then down the gullet into the first stomach. Kneeling behind him David Wild watched through the eyepiece as the tip of the instrument moved onwards, spraying the lens with water when stomach juices threatened to cloud the vision and pushing the walls of the stomach away from the tube with air so that he could have space to look around. Through a side attachment to the eye-piece Andrew was able to monitor progress as well. Before long they both saw the first of a series of ugly bleeding ulcers in the stomach lining. Everywhere there was black blood from the ulcers, partly digested. Brandy's digestion was in a terrible state. David swung the tip of the gastroscope round, and there was the ring! They could see a segment of the red plastic lying in a black pool of blood. The natural contractions of the stomach muscles against the hardening ring were grinding one ulcer after another through the delicate velvety lining of the organ.

Now to get the ring out. A special attachment to the gastroscope allowed the introduction of a wire loop which was guided round the ring and back to the gastroscope again. When the ring was firmly snared it was pulled to the tip of the instrument and then both ring and gastroscope were withdrawn together. Brandy gave an enormous gulp as the ring travelled back up his gullet. Luckily dolphins have remarkably elastic gullets for swallowing large fish whole, otherwise there would have been a risk of rupturing the organ. With the ring

75

gone Brandy looked much relieved, but Andrew reintroduced the gastroscope to inspect the ulcer damage. Some of the worst bleeding points were electrically cauterised and photographs were taken. Then Brandy was returned, to his great relief, to the pool and his wives, and his complete recovery was ensured by a course of tablets normally given to dyspeptic middle-aged business executives. To celebrate his sense of well-being after the poolside operation, Brandy was seen to mate long and amorously with one of the female dolphins, and eleven and a half months later, on the following Boxing Day, a little baby dolphin was born in the pool at Palma Nova.

Nine

Even stranger jobs than saving a drowning hippo or emptying a sealion of gravel have come my way. Arnold was a bloody-minded and malevolent African grey parrot with a powerful liking for the flesh of human fingers, a black hatred of dogs, particularly of Bimbo, the amiable and pacific retriever that lived in the same household, and a remarkable talent for vocal mimicry. Arnold had a pornographer's vocabulary but he did not limit himself to impersonating only human speech. He was also superb as a vacuum cleaner and as the clatter of the cover on the letter box. His *pièce de résistance*, however, was the characteristic click and squeak of the refrigerator door being opened. Arnold used his talent with what I can only describe as grim malice aforethought. When he had had a particularly liverish day, when perhaps the doting mother of the family had neglected to produce his customary after-lunch teaspoonful of Advocaat or the window cleaner had pulled faces at him, Arnold would take it out on Bimbo – indirectly, of course. Bimbo may have been rather dumb but he valued his hide too dearly to go within a yard of the parrot cage and its choleric occupant with the red-rimmed eyes and assiduously sharpened bill.

In the past Bimbo had occasionally been guilty of flicking open the refrigerator door in search of goodies, but he had been duly chastised and was now fully rehabilitated into society, a reformed character. When Arnold and Bimbo were alone in the living room and the parrot could see that the kitchen where the ice-box stood was also empty, that malign bird would loudly imitate the opening of the refrigerator door.

Immediately he would scream loudly 'Bimbo's at the chops, mother!' or 'The bloody dog's got the weekend joint, for Christ's sake!' The response, sadly, to this display of dastardly misrepresentation was predictable, unvarying. A member of the family ensconced in the parlour watching telly would emerge and boot Bimbo roughly out of the back door, invariably without checking whether the psittacine accusation was true or not. It did Arnold's black heart good to witness the affair, particularly if it was raining and he could watch the luckless dog standing dejectedly in the yard.

But the meek shall inherit the earth. Time ran out for Arnold. He was caught several times in the act of perjury by the family, who resented being hauled away from 'Coronation Street', and his bad language became positively disgusting. Mother had loved Arnold dearly since an old sailor boy friend had brought him as a present thirty years before, but it was decided that he would have to stop the ventriloquism. They came to me with Arnold and asked me to make him dumb.

Arnold took an instant dislike to me and I cannot say that he exactly turned me on, but I refused the request. To render animals voiceless by surgical techniques which take chunks out of their vocal chords is mutilation that can rarely be justified. There may be a point in silencing mules used for transporting military supplies in jungle terrain, as was done by the army in the Far East during the last war, but I have never agreed with the idea of removing the screeches or hoots or Arnoldian language from creatures, particularly exotic ones, just for the convenience of an owner who acquired them without first considering all the aspects of keeping such animals in captivity. Many owners of birds of prey or peafowl enjoy the appearance and activity of the birds but object to the natural noises that go with them: the eerie wail of a peacock at dead of night may put the wind up the more imaginative of your neighbours but if you and they cannot come to terms about having such gorgeous birds on your property, don't ask me to insert red hot cautery needles into the peacocks' voice boxes to destroy the source of the noise. People have even asked me to obliterate the honking of sealions by surgery. To them as to Arnold's owners I gave my stock reply: 'If you don't like the voice you shouldn't be keeping the animal.'

There have been much more bizarre requests. Tigers in the wild are fairly solitary beasts. Unlike lions they do not consort with their prides. After the success of the first safari parks, where lions adapted well, the constant entrepreneurial search for something new turned towards the idea of a tiger or leopard reserve, but there were fears that a group of tigers kept in a relatively small area might slaughter one another mercilessly in battles over artificial territory. With tigers worth ten times as much as lions such prospects deterred many park owners for some years. One English businessman was anxious to be the first to exhibit a big group of tigers living peacefully together and he asked me to meet him to discuss his idea of how it might be done. It was quite simple, he said as we sat in his walnut-panelled office sipping gin and tonics. All we had to do was to remove aggressive impulses from the minds of the tigers – make 'em placid and disinclined to squabble. It was, after all, being done all the time in mental hospitals and institutions for the criminally insane. He had read about it in *Reveille* and seen something on television. So why not do it in tigers? It was all quite simple: just perform a lobotomy on every tiger before introducing it into the reserve!

Imagine. The idea was to drill a hole in each tiger's skull and then to insert special neurosurgical saws to cut off the frontal lobe of the brain, to separate the 'personality' of the animal from the other functions of the brain which were essential for basic living. I marvelled at the man's sheer, stupid audacity in even conceiving such a plan. Apart from the need for highly delicate surgery of a kind never before undertaken in creatures of such a size, its precise effects would be unpredictable and irreversible. It had been performed experimentally on domestic cats in the laboratory but they were at least contributing to the serious scientific study of mental disorders in man.

What was being proposed to me was the creation of a pack of tiger zombies, orange and black striped organisms that would feed and breathe, defecate and sneeze, walk and stretch out in the sunshine for the benefit of carloads of paying punters, but would be no more tigers than the colourful paper models of Chinese New Year. It was a frightening proposition.

Even if it were legal, which I doubt, the last thing I would want to deal with is a Frankensteinesque tiger which has been tamed artificially by surgery. I have tiger friends who are gentle and fond of certain human beings because they have been brought up that way and there are others whom I greatly respect and who give me lots of trouble when I am called to examine or treat them. At least I understand their reluctance to be poked and pricked by people like me, and their indignation when restrained in a crush cage, for they are real, complete, magnificent animals. If I should become careless and drop my guard when examining an unanaesthetised wild animal, then I am quite rightly rewarded by a claw hooking my Achilles tendon through the bars or a horn smacked painfully into my backside. I do not want vegetable animals.

My meeting with the businessman lasted about three minutes, just long enough for him to describe his idea and for me to tell him what abominable nonsense it was.

Another businessman, wanting to cash in on the publicity for the Loch Ness monster, approached me with a different kind of request. Instead of faking up a 'monster' from plastic or canvas or upturned boats or oil drums he wanted to have a real live monster swimming in the loch and available for capture before the lenses of the world's breathless media men.

'I want to make a monster out of a big sealion or elephant seal,' he confided. 'If I get hold of a really big sealion will you stitch a plastic dragon's wing along the length of its back?'

He actually wanted me to suture a tall, spiky contraption painted in fearsome black and red to the delicate skin and thick blubber of a living creature. The wing had been made before he even mentioned his scheme to me. When I gave my reply, again brief and to the point, he became angry and spiteful.

'You vets may be all right with all this medical stuff but you'll never make any money. No commercial sense. All book learning and science. No idea of business.'

The meeting ended abruptly.

The possibility of the existence of a real Loch Ness monster has always fascinated me. The circumstantial evidence seems remarkably strong in favour of some type of large, possibly plesiosaur-like animal inhabiting the black depths of this immense stretch of water. Over the years I have been in touch with both scientists and lay people interested in various aspects of the monster problem. Folk who have been within six yards of the beast both in the water and on land and who have claimed to have infallible means of capturing, killing, biopsying, photographing or otherwise identifying the monster have asked me to join their expeditions.

There was the Dutchman who was certain he could kill the monster by setting a net studded with hand-grenades right across the loch and driving the creature to its doom by noise-making machines. There was the American who wanted me to help design an underwater dart fired from a spear-gun which would take a blood sample for later analysis so that we could identify the animal at our leisure from its blood protein characteristics. It seemed to be asking a lot to expect a dart to be fired underwater accurately into a blood vessel of an animal about whose anatomy no-one knows much.

'Ah, but it's bound to have a jugular vein!' enthused the American.

He had never seen the murky gloom that faces anyone swimming underwater in the loch, like being submerged in a vat of flat brown ale. Anyway I would not rely on being able to dart the jugular vein of, say, a crocodile or a hippopotamus on land in the most favourable conditions. Then there was the Englishman who wanted me to drive the monsters to the surface of the loch by a method used in Japan to catch dolphins. A long pole with a flat plate on the bottom end is pushed down into the water. The end of the pole above water is then hammered by the fisherman to produce irritating metallic noises underwater, a terrible din which causes the dolphins to rise, presumably with their ears ringing. It might work if the monsters have got sensitive ears but the Englishman could only afford to sponsor an expedition lasting one day!

'But we'll have one by lunchtime,' he said, pressing me to join his group.

More seriously, I have studied carefully all the written records of monster sightings at Loch Ness and in some other waters and have spoken to several people of integrity, teachers, clergymen and professional men, who claim actually to have seen the beast. The theoretical biological and ecological implications of the monster's existence interest me particularly. Being specially concerned with marine mammals I have studied the evidence to see whether the monster might have similarities to a freshwater seal or dolphin, possibly of the type that still exists in the Tung Ting Hu Lake in China and elsewhere. Like most scientists who have looked objectively at the problem I have come to the conclusion that a more likely candidate is a reptile, or possibly a warm-blooded dinosaur, with many similarities to the apparently extinct plesiosaur.

Certainly it must be carnivore, eating fish and particularly the eels which abound in the loch. There just is not enough vegetable matter in the lake's rather forbidding waters and the evidence suggests that land visits are infrequent and probably out of character. Martin Padley, the Flamingo Park whale trainer, and I had for some time been toying with the idea of making a bait suitable for a carnivorous reptile. It would have a strong, attractive underwater smell and would be fortified with hormones which are active in high dilution and which have a sexually stimulating effect on reptiles. The opportunity to try out our bait came when Independent Television, in conjunction with the Loch Ness Investigation Bureau, the Royal Navy (noise-making machines), the Plessey Company (underwater detection apparatus and two mini-subs), Birmingham University (sonar scanning) and many other experts from Britain and the United States, mounted a two-week expedition to sort out the elusive 'Nessie' once and for all. Martin and I were asked to join the expedition, both to conduct baiting experiments and to take along the dart-gun and a selection of knock-out drugs. This was a Loch Ness expedition I was prepared to join.

Before setting out for the north of Scotland we prepared our bait. It was, as Vincent Mulchrone of the *Daily Mail* was later to describe it, 'a foul-smelling black pudding'. We bought hundreds of pounds of dried blood, anchovy paste and gelatine. Sawdust was used as a filler. The ingredients, including small quantities of the reptile hormone, were mixed into a dark red jelly moulded in plastic buckets. When they had set, the contents of the buckets were put in plastic bags and loaded into the boot of my car.

By the time we had driven up to Inverness through boiling hot weather the giant raspberry-coloured 'lollipops' in the boot were beginning to smell ripely even through the plastic. If the strong fishy-bloody smell was as powerful underwater as it was on land and evoked a positive response in the monster population, they should come rushing from miles around! We unloaded the bait at the ITV base on the shores of the loch near Drumnadrochit. The place was teeming with newspapermen, television engineers, scientists of one discipline or another, skin divers, submariners and crowds of sightseers. In the first few minutes after our arrival excitement reached fever pitch. Two men had come into the camp with what looked like some great pre-historic monster's thigh bone which they claimed to have found nearby. The television people went wild about it. It was massive, obviously fossilized bone, and you could see the head of the femur, the bony projections and the holes for blood vessels. They had struck oil on the first day of the expedition!

Film was rushed to Inverness for 'News at Ten' and vast sums of cash were paid to the two bone finders for portions to be scientifically analysed. There was only one problem. Surprisingly, among all the experts of one sort or another at the lochside headquarters there was not one single person with biological training until I arrived. The TV producer and the journalists besieged me in a frenzy once they knew they had found someone familiar with animal anatomy. Would I please examine the monster thigh bone as a matter of urgency and pronounce upon it in front of the camera? I went to look at the find. It was about four feet high, weighing perhaps 150 pounds, definitely bone but greatly weathered rather than fossilized. I recognized it at once. Bones like it were often made into gate arches in places like Whitby and the Orkneys. It was part of a whale's lower jawbone.

Certainly there was a knobbly articulating surface at the thick end, but it fits into the upper jaw, not the pelvis. There were not tooth holes as giveaways since the bone came from a toothless species of baleen whale, the mighty blue. The television team, already in a state of high excitement, became ecstatic when I pronounced the find to be bone rather than fossilized wood. A well-known TV science correspondent stood it on end and pointed out the monster blood vessel apertures ('Surely the femoral artery emerged here!') and the bit where the thigh would join and support a pelvis that must have belonged to an animal weighing fifteen tons or more and adapted to wading in water. When I managed to get another word in edgeways I revealed what the bone really was. Sudden gloom descended and the television team, grown silent and wan, moved off as one man to the Drumnadrochit Hotel for restoratives. Later it was found that the 'monster bone' was identical to one which was missing from the garden of a museum in York.

When we got back to our dried-blood bait, the warm weather was continuing to produce an understandable effect. Nobody would come within fifty yards of us and we were attracting the attention of half the fly population of the north of Scotland. We loaded the bait, ten pounds at a time, into muslin bags.

These were to be suspended from buoys in areas of the loch where monster sightings had been most frequent. We were also going to groundbait an area of the loch with the stuff at a point where batteries of both fixed and shipboard sonar equipment would be scanning. In addition, the monsters would be driven into this area by boats carrying noise machines and moving up from either end of the loch. Only the sonar-covered, baited area would remain free of noise. With any luck this is where the monsters would arrive as the noise-makers approached one another. I, together with my dart-gun and dozens of photographers and TV cameras, would wait silently on a launch moored in the centre of the target area and surrounded by water redolent with the special bait.

There had been some problems in deciding my duties as anaesthetist/marksman. A strong Scottish conservationist element was breathing terrible threats of what would happen should the monster be inadvertently killed. How was I to calculate my dose for the flying syringe when I had no idea of species or weight? A biopsy would enable us to identify the creature and I had experimented using the syringe needles as biopsy samplers, recovering the darts by means of very strong but fine nylon line attached to the missile before firing. I was not impressed: the technique was clumsy and unreliable. In the end I decided to dart any monster that made an appearance with valium, a tranquilliser which is effective in a very wide range of wild animals but which would not produce anaesthesia and possible death if the monster dived below the surface. Perhaps a tranquillised Nessie would be more forthcoming and lose some of her obsessive shyness.

On the day of the big sweep the noise-makers came slowly towards us, while I stood on the prow of the launch looking down at the black water and Martin bobbed about in a dinghy scattering dried-blood bait onto the waves as an extra enticement. Everyone was in position. Anything moving underwater at any depth in the silent target zone would be picked up and recorded on the sonar tapes. Somewhere in the black water beneath our launch lurked out two one-man submarines carrying powerful searchlights and cameras. They should be the first to catch a glimpse of the monsters. Then, so the planning ran, the animals would break the surface just over there, a few yards from where I stood, and within a few minutes the dozens of cameras mounted on the launch and the other boats would prove once and for all the nature of Scotland's most famous inhabitant. It was foolproof and precise, according to the Director of Operations. Any monster was bound to surface in camera for the benefit of the TV people. Nessie, for the first time in a millennia of her existence, was about to be produced.

With our hearts in our mouths we saw the noise-making boats reach their final positions just outside the target area and stop. There was not a sound as we stared intently at the small area of choppy water where the monster must now be lying. Cameramen focused on the water surface where Nessie must surely now emerge. I aimed my rifle at the spot. There was a loaded syringe up the spout and the safety catch was off. Then, breaking the silence, the radio telephone laconically announced that the sonar scanners could find nothing in the area. The monsters had failed to co-operate. We would try again, but next time at night.

The expedition persevered but Nessie either snoozed in her underwater caverns or cared not a fig for the puny noise-maker brought along by the Navy. Just before we left Loch Ness at the end of the venture we used the remainder of our bait in bags attached to free-floating oil drums. The drifting drums would be kept under observation by the members of the Investigation Bureau who manned strategic points on the banks of the loch throughout the summer and autumn. Some days later when we were back in England we received a report that the crew of a fishing boat, the *Snowdrop*, passing through the loch on their way to the Caledonian Canal, had been frightened out of their wits by two monsters apparently fighting over a yellow oil drum. It would be nice to think that the beasts were squabbling over the free meal which we had cooked up for them.

Undoubtedly the most exciting aspect of zoo animal medicine is that concerning birth. Most exotic creatures have little trouble in giving birth to their young and although there are fertility problems in many species, obstetric complications are rare. It is always a privilege to be able to witness the birth of a young chimpanzee or antelope or dolphin, but to be called on to give assistance in a difficult labour has a magic of its own. The mothers almost always seem to understand that you are there to give a hand and rarely, even with the wildest species, react badly when you get down to brass tacks at their rear ends. I have never been kicked by a giraffe or wildebeest as I have followed it around with my arm deep inside the womb straightening out the knotted legs and badly positioned head of a wriggling calf that has jammed on the way out. For giraffes there is usually a man carrying an orange-box for me to stand on. The straining mother moves slowly about her pen. When she stops the box is placed for me and, with an arm coated in lubricant antiseptic jelly, I feel inside to determine the problem. If I pull the calf's limb or head the mother will normally push and bear down with her powerful abdominal muscles, but if she moves on I quickly jump off the box and chase after her with my assistant. Getting someone to feed the mother pieces of brown bread on such occasions is a considerable help.

All the baby dolphins I have been called to see so far have arrived speedily and unaided. My only difficult dolphin birth was one where my patient and I were 1400 miles apart: an animal in Malta was having great difficulty giving birth and I conducted the calving over the telephone. A nurse and the local government vet worked on the dolphin while an assistant standing at the telephone at the side of the pool relayed my instructions. After exchanging information and advice to and fro continuously for about three quarters of an hour, I was relieved to hear above the crackle and hum on the wires the sudden cries of delight from the midwives as the pointed head of the baby dolphin at last came free.

Occasionally I have to give the mother an anaesthetic in order to tackle a more complicated delivery snarl-up, as in the case of a powerfully built zebra belonging to Flamingo Park Zoo in Yorkshire. The keepers had seen afterbirth hanging from her for some hours and assumed that she had foaled and that the foal was somewhere in the zebra reserve, but a careful search revealed nothing. I was called in and examined the nervous animal at a distance through binoculars. She still had the afterbirth dangling. The fact that her tummy was rounded and bulging did not necessarily mean that a foal was still in there, as zebras' shapes can be very deceptive. Then I saw her stand and lift the floor of her abdomen in a long, powerful contraction. A small white object appeared outside the birth canal and then popped back in again as she stopped straining. It was the delicate little hoof of the baby zebra emerging under pressure. I decided to leave well alone for two hours and then re-assess the position. Two hours later I returned to the zebra reserve. Peering through the binoculars I saw no sign of straining, although the baby had still not been born. No part of the foal was visible and the mother seemed to be duller and more tired. All was not going well, and I decided to intervene.

Because the animal could not be closely approached I would use the long-range dart-gun. I had found that it was possible to get closer to groups of deer, antelope and zebra by taking vehicles into their large paddocks rather than by going in on foot, so I decided to take my car in and shoot from that. At the time I had a Citroën saloon whose adjustable suspension made riding at speed over rough ground and firing a rifle at the same time, as if from a Western stagecoach, fairly easy. A keeper drove my car towards the mother-to-be and when in range I pulled the trigger. The syringe thwacked into her buttocks and she moved a few paces, flicking at it with her tail. The missile hits so fast that it produces no more pain than a smack of a hand so the target rarely runs off in alarm. Five minutes later the zebra was asleep on the ground and I began my internal examination. The foal was terribly tangled up with itself and I could detect no sign of life in it. Although I could unravel the awkwardly bent legs, struggle as I might I could not position correctly the foal's head, which was bent backwards deep into the womb and also twisted round on itself. The mother's natural lubricating liquids were drying up. I had no choice but to try a Caesarean operation.

Caesareans in the horse family, of which the zebra is a member, are still not common. Horses were at one time far greater risks for this type of operation than cattle or sheep, since they get peritonitis after abdominal surgery at the drop of a hat and until the development of modern anaesthetics and antibiotics did not have much of a chance: even today there are unsolved problems in major abdominal surgery of the horse. Cattle, on the other hand, have a tough constitution and an abdominal cavity whose design resists the onset of peritonitis, while Caesarean operations on domestic animals are of course very common. In fact, the first successful operation on the bitch was carried out as long ago as 1824, by a vet in my home town of Rochdale. In zoo animals Caesareans are quite often performed on the big cats and on primates, but on zebras and other exotic horses nothing had been done before this case. But I had no option. I had to open her up.

A tractor pulled the sleeping zebra into the stable on a sledge improvised from an old door. For a large animal like this there is rarely a spotless, aseptic operating theatre at hand so we have to operate literally in the field. After reinforcing the anaesthesia by numbing the belly with local anaesthetic I cut quickly through the skin and muscle and peritoneal tissues, bringing the bulging uterus into the light of day. As usual with wild animals there was none of the messy fat tissue which clogs up the operation site in so many obese and pampered pets. I opened the womb and the striped leg of the foal popped out. Perhaps there was still a flicker of life. I pulled, and the slim and perfect form of the baby zebra slid out onto the side of its unconscious dam. Ignoring the mother for the moment I quickly opened her foal's mouth and hooked the mucus out of its throat with my fingers. Then I took it by its hind fetlocks and whirled it round and round my body as fast as possible, trying to clear its breathing tubes by centrifugal force. I stopped and listened. If its heart was beating I could not detect it. I gave an injection of stimulant and dropped some liquid on the back of the tiny tongue to kick the breathing centres into action. Still nothing. Finally I tried mouth to mouth respiration, packing the slippery little muzzle into my mouth and blowing as hard as I could. It was no use. The foal could not respond. It was dead.

The mother still had to be saved for her next son. I scrubbed up again and went back to work stitching up the layers in the operation wound. Before closing the abdomen I left behind in the peritoneal cavity a handful of antibiotic tablets and sprayed the bowels with a chemical to stop peritonitis sticking them together. Finally I sutured the tough skin, tearing my fingers as I gripped the large curved needles with their cutting edges. Finished. The zebra was breathing strongly. Surprisingly little blood had been lost during the operation, hardly more than a tablespoonful. I gave her a precautionary dose of antibiotics injected into her neck, then the anaesthetic antidote. Two minutes later she snorted, righted herself, rose and walked sedately out to the reserve. I was happy to see her go, for the reserve was a cleaner place for post-operative recovery than a dusty stable.

The zebra never looked back. She recovered superbly from the operation without the slightest hint of complications. The following year she was proudly to produce unaided and unobserved the most charming little zebra filly one could wish to see.

Ten

'Can you go out straightaway to Pakistan?' the question came over the telephone. 'There's a chap near the border with Afghanistan who claims he's got pigmy sperm whales.'

I was accustomed to all manner of unusual requests from Pentland Hick, the owner of Flamingo Park in Yorkshire and of the zebra on which I had just performed the first Caesarean operation in the species. An expert entomologist and a pioneer of the boom in displays of performing dolphins in Europe, he was an entrepreneur of imagination and audacity. He was always looking for new ideas in animal exhibition, and was responsible for Cuddles, the first killer whale to be brought to England. He was also responsible for my initiation into the fascinating world of marine mammal medicine: realising that medical care and water management were the keys to the successful management of porpoises, dolphins and whales, he sent me all over the world, but most importantly to the United States on several occasions, to learn at first hand about the catching, handling and water requirements of these amazing creatures. It was through his enthusiastic support that I spent time with the undersea warfare division of the US Navy, and went clambering about the ice floes of Greenland in search of the strange unicorn of the sea, the narwhal. Now here was Pentland Hick off on yet another tack.

Kogia breviceps, the pigmy sperm whale, is a charming miniaturisation of the cachalot or sperm whale. Never growing much above seven feet in length, as compared to the sperm whale's length of fifty to sixty feet, it appears to be widely distributed throughout the oceans of the world although it is very rarely seen by man. It tends to swim alone or in small groups and feeds on squid and probably crabs. Virtually nothing is known about its habits or reproduction, but the facts that it was small, weighed only 600 to 700 pounds, and would therefore be easy to transport, and that it had teeth and preferred food which is readily available in Britain, made it a suitable and exciting prospect for Hick's expanding collection of cetacean species. Two other small whales on which we were working at the time, the beluga and the narwhal, needed refrigeration equipment to keep the temperature of their pool down to Arctic levels. Kogia seemed to be a frequenter of much more temperate waters and therefore easier to keep.

The man who had written to Pentland Hick with the offer of pigmy sperm whales was unknown to us. He was apparently a Scottish naturalist living in Quetta, the provincial capital of Baluchistan, and dealing in birds and animals of that part of the world which he claimed to supply to zoos in various countries. His name, let us say, was McPherson. Apart from friends at the Steinhart Aquarium in San Francisco who said that they had met a man of that name while collecting freshwater dolphins in Pakistan some weeks earlier, I could find no-one in the zoo or animal business who had heard of him. Still, his letter stated plainly and without ambiguity that he had got *Kogia breviceps* for sale and at a reasonable price.

'I want you to go out as soon as possible and see what McPherson has got to offer,' said Hick. 'We can't afford to run the risk of anyone else in Europe beating us to it.'

As soon as possible was the next day. I booked my flight to Karachi by radio telephone while driving back from Flamingo Park to Rochdale. One thing that puzzled me when I got back and consulted the atlas was that Quetta is situated hundreds of miles from the sea in the rugged hills of the north-west frontier – an unusual base for whale-catching. I could not recall any reference to such goings-on in those stirring films that featured Errol Flynn and his lancers.

I flew out to Karachi via Moscow on PIA, a thoroughly

miserable flight; within thirty minutes of leaving Heathrow almost all the passengers had been air-sick. After a brief rest in Karachi I took off again, this time in a small and rather ancient aeroplane, for Quetta. The passenger sitting next to me was a pleasant but loquacious character with a brother in England whom, he felt sure, I must have met. He was carrying a block of what looked like fudge wrapped in silver paper and weighing about three pounds. It was high-quality cannabis resin and mine to take home as a souvenir for a mere twenty pounds, my companion suggested. After all, he posted it regularly to his brother in Birmingham. I tried to disengage from the conversation by concentrating on the view through the aircraft window as we flew north over red desert country but my neighbour had not finished with me yet. After downing the best part of a pint of whisky from a bottle he produced from his bag, he was apologetically sick all over my trousers. The Pakistan adventure was not beginning well.

The red desert suddenly gave way to a mountainous grey lunar landscape. Valleys and peaks looked uniformly sterile and forbidding, unrelieved by any streams or trees or signs of habitation. As we came in to land at the airfield which serves Quetta, the resemblance to the moon surface was even more striking. We glided down onto a grim grey plateau, the centre of a vast crater in the middle of the mountains. Apart from a small building that served as the air terminal nothing but pallid dust could be seen in any direction. Having collected my bags and discovered that the hotel in Quetta to which PIA in Manchester had cabled to reserve a room for me had been pulled down five years earlier, I found myself standing alone in the dusk outside the terminal wondering where to go and how. Apparently there was no way of getting into the town, some miles away. Apart from the man in the tiny control tower, who did not seem interested in opening his door or window to discover what it was I kept shouting at him, there was no-one about. The aircraft had taken off for its next destination, Peshawar, and the light was beginning to fade.

Just then a decrepit old station wagon came rattling down the road. It was tightly packed with fierce-looking Pathans and an assortment of skinny goats and sheep. Desperate to get moving, I ran out into the road and flagged the vehicle down. It stopped and I scrambled thankfully into the tight press of smelly animals. The men said not a word to me and hardly cast a glance in my direction. It was as if they had not noticed the addition to their load. We rumbled off in clouds of dust and eventually arrived at the town. When the wagon stopped in a narrow street of dilapidated wooden shacks and stinking open sewers, I got out and thanked the driver, who drove on without acknowledging my farewells in any way. By this time I was very dishevelled and reeked of an outlandish mixture of human vomit and goat.

It was a long time before I found someone who spoke English and who could direct me to the only hotel in Quetta, a decaying wooden relic of the British Empire called, of all things, the Regina Coeli. An unprepossessing character, unshaven and with a wall eye, who spoke a little English, informed me that I would be their sole guest and showed me to the filthest suite of rooms I have ever seen. Darkness had fallen and it had grown bitterly cold. My host brought a home-made metal stove and set it up in my room. He explained its intricacies and temperamental ways and sold me a quantity of oil for it at an astronomical price. By the light of its noisy, fluctuating flame I was able, once I was alone, to explore the four rooms I had been given, including a lavatory built directly over an evil cesspit. There were doors everywhere, behind which I could hear people shuffling about and murmuring. Whoever they were they seemed to be constantly on the threshold of the other side of the doors. It was eerie and disturbing. With much difficulty, for apart from a low wooden bed and the stove there was not a scrap of furniture in the rooms, I secured all the entrances with bits of wood or stone wedged under the doors. I closed the shutters and wired them so that they could not be opened from outside and went to bed.

As I lay on the low bed I noticed an irregular pattern of red dots decorating the crumbling white plaster of the walls. It was difficult to tell what they were by the light of the stove so I struck a match for closer inspection. They were the bloody patches where countless fingers had squashed bed bugs into oblivion. I could see the thumbprints and the fragments of corpses ground into the plaster. Thoroughly dismayed I got up and took the cowl off the stove. The flames soared up to the ceiling and coated it with oily soot. Now I could see better. I had never actually met *Cimex lectularius*, the bed bug, in person but I had studied him and his kind when doing my Fellowship and knew where he was likely to be found. Sure enough, from the cracks in the dry rot of the skirting board and from wide cracks in the wall plaster, like climbers from a rock chimney, the flat and unmistakable insects were beginning to emerge. I stripped the bed, found and eradicated more of them. Finally, with oil from the stove I made shallow pools on the stone floor round the bed legs and painted a strip of oil round all four walls to prevent my unwelcome companions from climbing up to the ceiling and launching parachute attacks. Exhausted and miserable, cold and damp, still smelling of goat and other things, I eventually fell asleep fully clothed on the top of the bed.

A peep into the kitchen the following morning and I decided to fast for as long as I was in the hotel. The cook thought it most strange that I would take nothing but tea and that without milk. Hunger was now added to my miseries, but I was reluctant to share their repast with the two enormous brown rats that I had just seen sitting in a cooling pan of vegetables and eating unhurriedly from the warm pottage in which they reclined.

My job was to find McPherson and his pigmy sperm whales and then to get out of Quetta with all speed. Finding him proved to be almost impossible. The hotel owner knew of no Englishman or Scot with such a name in the town. He could not think of any Europeans in the place at all, except for the strange young people who passed through from time to time on their way from Afghanistan to India: Quetta is a watering place on the twentieth-century pilgrims' way. I went into the town past the derelict barracks and rusting cannon still bearing the names of famous British regiments, down streets lined by windowless wooden dwellings as small as police boxes and with sacks for doors, and across weedy fields where white mosques gleamed against the grey backdrop of the mountains. Quetta looks like what it in fact is, a frontier town. It was devastated by an earthquake in 1935 and has never recovered. I found the police station, the office of the agriculture ministry and the municipal headquarters. No-one had heard of McPherson nor of any naturalists working in the area. As for whales, even the English-speaking people that I met did not understand the meaning of the word. When I drew a picture of a whale to make matters clearer their eyes opened wide and they looked at me curiously. 'But the sea is far away, sir,' said one puzzled policeman.

All day I wandered through the town looking for clues to the whereabouts of McPherson. Knots of tall, striking-looking Baluch tribesmen standing on the corners found me an object of great curiosity and some amusement as I tried to orientate myself with the aid of a street map of 1940 vintage. McPherson's letter naturally bore an address. Not only could I not find the street on my map, but no-one I spoke to admitted any knowledge of such a place. The day ended with me no nearer finding the elusive naturalist but my hunger was growing and the weather was becoming colder, threatening rain. I spent another unhappy night at the hotel fortified only by tea and lay awake most of the night as a great storm swept down from the mountains and the wind threatened to blow the building away.

Off I went round the town again the next morning. I was becoming convinced that McPherson was some sort of confidence trickster trying to extract money by false pretences from Pentland Hick. Perhaps he had been hoping to obtain a deposit in advance. But in that case why pick on Quetta as a supposed

96

base for his marine operations? And if the address was false, as seemed likely, how could money sent by mail possibly reach him? I decided to try the post office again. The day before I had drawn a blank but surely if the man or his address had ever existed in Quetta he must have received post. I went into the post office building and stood looking at the rows of numbered post boxes. Someone tapped me on my shoulder. I looked round to find a large, smartly dressed policeman with a swagger stick confronting me.

'Dr Taylor, sir?' he enquired politely. 'I wonder if you would be kind enough to come with me. My Superintendent would like to meet you.'

He led me out to his jeep. A fat man with bloodshot eyes and a nude blonde painted on his tie sat silently in the back seat. We bounced through the rough, rubble-strewn streets and stopped outside a tall building covered with peeling pink paint. The policeman led me inside and the fat man followed behind. We entered an office where another policeman sat at a desk and a civilian wearing gumboots on a settee against one wall. The man behind the desk smiled, introduced himself as the Superintendent and asked me to sit down. This must be something to do with the guy on the plane, I thought, my sick friend with the cannabis.

'Dr Taylor, I have asked you to come in to see us,' the Superintendent began, 'because we believe you are having difficulties finding an acquaintance of yours.'

Very civil, I thought, perhaps they have located him for me. 'Yes,' I said, 'Mr McPherson, the naturalist.'

The man with bloodshot eyes grunted loudly. There was silence for a few moments.

'McPherson, the naturalist.' The Superintendent repeated my words slowly as if reflecting on them. 'Are you here to see him on business or on pleasure?'

'Business. I'm up here to see him about whales. I'm a veterinary surgeon.'

Now the fat bloodshot individual grunted again and spoke

97

for the first time. 'Dr Taylor, a veterinary surgeon, eh? An animal doctor from England, eh? To see McPherson the naturalist, eh?'

'Yes indeed,' I replied, beginning to feel a little uneasy. 'Why? Is there something odd about that?'

The Superintendent spoke again. 'This is Major Darwish,' he said, indicating the fat man, 'Major Darwish of Military Security.'

For the next hour I sat while Major Darwish explained the reason for this interview. There was political trouble in Baluchistan, moves for regional autonomy, even secession. It was a sensitive area, border problems, big power interest and so on. The Pakistan Government had detected American CIA activity in the border area based on Quetta. Some Americans had been asked to leave the country and McPherson was thought to be implicated in the whole business.

'We've got our eye on your Mr McPherson,' said Major Darwish, 'and we've got our eye on anyone who comes up here trying to fish in troubled waters. The tribal problems are delicate enough for Karachi without foreigners making matters worse.' He leaned forward towards me and spoke in a mock confidential tone. 'Do you know Quetta has been crawling with CIA men?'

The penny dropped. I had been hauled in as a possible agent of a foreign power!

'You don't think I'm a CIA man, do you?' I laughed, perhaps a shade too heartily.

There was silence, then the Superintendent said, 'But we are told, Dr Taylor, that you are an animal doctor looking for a man who has whales, that you have been enquiring around town as to where he lives and saying to people that you are here to inspect sea animals. We do not have whales or sea animals in Quetta. The sea is far away. And we are wishing to assure ourselves that what you tell us is right.'

'It is right,' I said with some annoyance. 'That's why I'm here.'

'We would like to be sure that you are indeed an animal doctor,' cut in Darwish. 'What university did you attend?'

I gave them a terse curriculum vitae and finished by saying that if they would produce a horse or a goat for a demonstration of my trade I would prove I was telling the truth by castrating it neatly on the spot.

'Well,' said Darwish, 'that won't be necessary. This gentleman is Dr Mohammed, a veterinary graduate of Lahore who works in the government service here.' He pointed to the man sitting silently in his gumboots. 'I think Dr Mohammed might ask you a couple of questions to validate your claim to be a veterinary surgeon. I'm sure you will understand.'

I was stunned. Here was I, suspected of being a spy in the fastnesses of the north-west frontier, about to be given a viva voce by another vet about whom I knew nothing. What if he had firm but erroneous opinions on some matter on which he questioned me? And was there not a good chance that he would ask me about some local malady about which I knew little or nothing? Dr Mohammed stood up importantly and cleared his throat.

'Now, sir,' he began with an air of great solemnity, 'would you kindly answer the following three questions. Firstly, what is the volume of the gall bladder in the mule? Secondly, for what do I use butter of antimony? And thirdly, what is Bang's disease?'

He sat down with a satisfied smile. Everyone looked at me. The first question was a trick one.

'Well, Dr Mohammed,' I said, 'the answer to the one about the gall bladder of the mule is that its volume is exactly the same as that of the dolphin's gall bladder.'

Dr Mohammed jumped to his feet with gleaming eyes. 'Aha,' he exclaimed, somewhat theatrically, 'you really will have to be more explicit than that. I asked you the volume. Approximately how many c.c.'s?'

'Like I said, the same as a dolphin or in other words, zero.' Horses and mules and whales and dolphins do not possess gall

99

bladders although they do produce bile and have bile ducts.

Mohammed sat down again looking a trifle crestfallen.

'The second question about butter of antimony is a bit old-fashioned,' I continued. 'I've not seen it used for years but it was applied to foot infections in cattle. Bang's disease is contagious brucella abortion.'

There was another long silence and then Darwish began a lengthy questioning of Dr Mohammed in Urdu. Eventually he turned to me.

'Dr Taylor, you may go, we are satisfied. We wish you well in your search for Mr McPherson.'

'But I assume you know where he is,' I said. 'You say you're keeping an eye on him. How do I find him?'

'I'm sorry,' replied the Superintendent. 'He was here but we don't know where he is now.'

Everyone looked a bit sheepish and I realised that my interview was over and that I was not going to get any more out of them. Thanking them I left the building and took a bicycle rickshaw back to the hotel. I would leave next morning for Karachi. McPherson had been the cause of a wild goose chase. Pigmy sperm whales indeed!

The hotel keeper said that there would be no flights out on the following day. The storms were still blowing in the mountains and the small aircraft could not make it over the high peaks encircling the town. In low spirits I sat in my room drinking tea and hungrier than ever. Somehow I felt that it might be worth one more try at finding McPherson, especially as I would have to spend at least another day in this dreary place anyway.

The next morning dawned grey and showery. Walking down into the town I puzzled over where to make more enquiries. As I stood looking round, a sign on a small bungalow across the road caught my eye. 'Ministry of Forests' it read. Perhaps they knew of naturalists going on expeditions in areas under their supervision. I went in and asked the first person I saw for the director. He got my meaning and took me through dim corridors cluttered with ragged figures squatting in corners and against walls. The Director of Forestry was a pleasant little man who spoke some English. To my delight, when I brought up the question of McPherson, the naturalist, I did not receive the expected blank look and shake of the head.

'I think I know who you mean,' he said. 'I'm not certain of the name but there is an Englishman.' He rang a bell and an assistant appeared. 'I'll get Hussein here to take you.'

I was elated. It looked as if I had done it at last. Hussein hailed a bicycle rickshaw and we climbed in. Through the middle of the town we went and into an area which I had not explored on foot. The streets became narrower and the tarmac gave way to dirt tracks between tightly packed wooden hovels. We rattled through a maze of muddy lanes where beggars crouched over open sewers and thin dogs covered with sores barked and howled. We were in the worst of the slums, surely on the wrong track. Abruptly we came upon the only proper building in the middle of that odorous shanty town, a dirty white bungalow that had known far better days and was surrounded by a high wall of dried mud. We stopped and paid off the rickshaw driver and knocked on the gate. After much barking of dogs it opened and a young man in baggy trousers whom I took to be a house-boy let us in. I explained why we were there and he took us into the house.

Inside it was dim and smoky. We were led into a large room that looked like a curio shop. Stuffed animals were piled around the walls, trinkets and weapons and articles of falconry equipment hung in clusters from the ceiling. Three hawks sat on blocks in the middle of the stone floor. In the light of the log fire, lying on a sofa drawn up close to the hearth, lay a European of about forty with tangled hair and a reddish beard. He was sleeping fully dressed in grubby clothes. His face was covered in big drops of sweat and his hands and arms were a mass of nasty sores. The house-boy gently roused the sleeping figure, who opened his eyes but made no attempt to rise.

'Good morning,' I said, as he blinked at me and wiped his eyes feebly. 'I'm Dr Taylor from Flamingo Park, England. Are you Mr McPherson by any chance?'

In a polished public-school accent he replied, 'I am, but I'm afraid I'm not well at present. You shouldn't have come out here until I asked you to come.'

His voice was weak and tired. The sores on his arms were going septic and the lymphatic channels stood out in dull red lines. I asked him what was wrong. Apparently he had been severely bitten by some falcons and was obviously at least on the brink of septicaemia. I always carry a selection of broad-spectrum antibiotics when visiting the East, so I gave him all the terramycin tablets I had. He accepted them gratefully. Apparently antibiotics were hard to come by and expensive, and it was clear that he was very short of cash. I told him I would give the antibiotics time to take effect and start reducing his fever, then I would return later in the day and talk with him.

After spending the day in the foothills outside the town I returned alone to McPherson's house with the aid of a scrap of paper on which his house-boy had written the directions for the rickshaw driver. McPherson was looking a bit better, sitting up and dressing his wounds. I got straight down to brass tacks – I had come to see his pigmy sperm whales. He had problems there, it appeared. The whales were six hundred miles away by the coast. Could I go down to see them? No, because he hadn't known I was arriving and would be unable to accompany me. Alone then? Well, no, that would be difficult.

I began to realise that my whole trip had been in vain. As we talked I found him anxious to discuss the financial aspects of the matter and keen to describe how he had trapped the animals, but gradually I pressed him to tell me precisely how many whales he actually had and exactly where. Of course he had none, nor did his catching facilities and holding pools seem to have much substance. He showed me photographs of sea-scapes and muddy estuaries but on none were there any traces of sea mammals. They could have been taken anywhere. He was adamant that he could not accompany me to the coast.

'I shall go alone and look around for myself,' I said.

'If only you had waited until I told you to come,' McPherson replied, 'I could have shown you pigmy sperms.'

He could not explain why his letter had so enthusiastically assured customers that the whales were ready and waiting for inspection. I asked him about Major Darwish and the CIA. He agreed that some of his friends had been expelled and showed me the Land Rover they had had to leave behind but he was reluctant to talk further about the matter or to tell me how and why he existed in such an odd place. Apart from the dogs and hawks there were no animals to be seen or heard.

Before I left to pack my bags McPherson said there was something else I might be interested in. What would Pentland Hick offer for a pair of giant pandas? It is impossible to put a price on this most popular and rare of exotic animals but I said that I was sure he would give a million pounds. McPherson had a scheme, on which he was shortly to embark, for smuggling pandas out of China. Would I like to join the expedition? The plan was breathtaking. A team of men, including me as vet to tranquillise the animals and watch their health, would leave Bangladesh (East Pakistan as it then was) and travel by mule and on foot across Assam, skirt the foothills of the Nyenchen-tanglha Mountains of Tibet and reach the panda country of Szechwan in China. The distance was about 850 miles over high uninhabited regions for the second half of the journey. The pandas would be brought back into Pakistan, dyed brown and shipped out as low-value brown bears! McPherson showed me the maps and other documents he had collected in preparation for the expedition.

'Will you join us?' he asked. 'It'll be worth £25,000 to you.'

'I'll wait until we've got some pigmy sperm whales first,' I said. 'Then I might consider it.'

Two days later the weather improved and I took a flight back to Karachi. I decided to visit the fishing villages on the coastline near the city to see what the fishermen knew about sea mammals in the area. My first call was to the offices of the Port Authorities where I asked about whale and dolphin catching by the fishing fleets.

'The fishermen take great pains not to catch or injure dolphins or whales,' the director explained. 'You would not find it possible to persuade them to help you.'

The fishing folk apparently consider cetaceans to be half human and therefore sacred. They base their belief on their knowledge that the sea mammals, unlike fish, produce milk to suckle their young and also make sounds similar to the human voice under certain conditions. What the director had said turned out to be true. I visited a number of primitive fishing communities on the salt flats north-west and south of the city, accompanied by a helpful employee of the Dutch airline KLM, who have a reputation for superb animal transporting facilities. I took with me a book of coloured illustrations of various species of sea mammal. The fact that the labelling and text was all in Japanese did not matter, as the man from KLM asked the fishermen just to point to pictures of any animals that they had ever encountered. I would stand in the middle of a cluster of dried mud dwellings while the people gathered round to stare at the pictures. Men at every village nodded when I pointed to the spinner dolphin. Some knew the pilot whale and the killer. At only one village could I find a man who had apparently seen a pigmy sperm whale and that only in deep water and very infrequently. They smiled and nodded at pictures of the dugong, probable origin of the mermaid myth. Yes, they were well acquainted with her and was she not a cross between man and dolphin? In one village the dugong picture brought much shuffling of feet and embarrassed lowering of heads. The KLM man said that they knew of fishermen who had taken dugong as lovers, but that they did not like to talk about it with strangers. Dugong were trouble. Their wives would scold them for days if they knew that they had even discussed them.

So pigmy sperm whales were not to be. Before leaving

Karachi for home I cabled McPherson to say that there was nothing doing at the coast. Just before I left my hotel to go to the airport he telephoned me from Quetta saying that he had some more of the elusive creatures in a set of ponds about twenty miles east of Karachi. If only I would wait a few days I would see. I was sceptical, but he protested vehemently that he could prove he was telling the truth. To my astonishment McPherson revealed that his house-boy, the young fellow who had let us into his house and stood quietly in the shadows during our conversations, was a qualified vet; McPherson had sent him down to the ponds near Karachi to look after the animals. If I looked over the side of a certain bridge near a Parsee fire temple I would see the animals and the house-boy in two large pools cut out of the rock. If he had had time he would have come down to Karachi to show me himself, he said, and pleaded with me to go to the pools before going home. I told him I would try, and bade him farewell.

Consulting my timetable, I worked out that I had just about enough time to make a forty-mile round trip by taxi before checking in for the flight to England, so off I set in a noisy Chevrolet with wheel wobble. The driver was a diminutive man who came originally from Goa and before letting out the clutch he informed me that he was, undoubtedly like myself, a Christian in an Islamic state. Also he had thirteen children, so would I ensure that his tip at the end of the journey was suitably lavish. I believe he was hinting that in doing so I would be actively supporting the conversion of Pakistan.

We reached the Parsee temple and the bridge. I got out and walked to the side. Below the bridge was a wide dried-out river bed. A number of holes had been scooped out of the rocky bank. Women washed clothes in murky green water from a drain that emptied onto the rocks above them, the liquid finding its way in a dozen trickling streams down to the pools, the solid matter being left behind on the stone to bake in the sunshine. Other women were spreading laundry on the rocks to dry. Two of the pools were much larger than the others and

105

were not being used. In the foul green water of one of them something floated half submerged.

I went down the rocks to the pool and looked at the dark shape hanging motionless in the water. It was a dead baby whale. Its umbilical cord could just be seen running down from the belly into the cloudy depths. There was a rusty old car spring on the ground not far away. I used it to pull in the corpse and flip it out onto the rocks. A new-born pigmy sperm whale! Unable to believe my eyes, I looked around. There was no sign of any other whales nor of McPherson's house-boy/vet nor of anything to suggest that this was the centre for a whale-catching operation. I examined the little body. It was a female and only the second member of the species that I had ever seen in the flesh. How had it got to this place? No-one seemed to take any notice as I began to do a makeshift autopsy on the spot with a penknife produced by the taxi driver. Two things I found that were of importance. One, the animal had not been born dead: it had breathed, for the lungs were fully expanded. Two, there was severe bruising, haemorrhage, splitting of flesh and scorching in the rectal area. The burnt-out case of a firework, the sort English boys call 'bangers', was jammed deep inside the anus.

My head spinning with rage and shock, numb with incomprehension, I was driven to the airport. The whole affair was bitter and bizarre. I never learned any more about that poor little soul, nor how it came to so cruel an end nor at whose hands. I have not heard any more from McPherson, nor to my knowledge has anyone else. I sent a final caustic cable to him in Quetta before leaving Karachi Airport but had no reply. About pigmy sperm whales in Pakistan we are no wiser, although some three months after I returned from this strange visit there arrived at Flamingo Park an unsigned cable that read 'PLEASE SEND FORTY YARDS STRONG TAPE FOR CONSTRUCTING CARRYING SLINGS PIGMY SPERMS URGENT'. The telegraph office of origin was Quetta.

Eleven

So little research has been done in exotic animal medicine compared to the other branches of veterinary science that a zoo vet must seize on any scraps of information which might help him in his work. Thus it was that I took my first lessons in the care of the camel from the manual of the Royal Army Veterinary Corps. Not much has been published about the health problems of camels, but somewhere I had found an ancient copy of this work and among the masses of information on unlikely things such as how to dispose of dead horses at sea and how many miles a pack mule can be expected to go on so many pounds of groundsel, I found what the Army knew about camels and their problems in days when military men considered such knowledge essential.

A camel in the Manchester Zoo which had been in England for almost three years was becoming thin and debilitated for no apparent reason. Try as I might I could not find any firm cause, and tonics, pick-me-ups and vitamins were not having much effect. After some weeks of illness swellings began to appear on the camel's sides and legs. The tissues in these regions were soggy: if you pushed your finger in you left a dent that stayed for hours as if in putty. The camel was developing dropsy. I checked and re-checked the heart, took urine samples for more tests of kidney function, and sent blood to the laboratory for analysis of liver function. But no, the dropsy was coming from none of the expected sources. There did not seem to be much wrong with heart, liver or kidneys.

The case puzzled me. I read what little I could find in the

pathology books I had available without getting much further. One day I remembered that the Army manual had talked about certain important diseases and I vaguely recalled something about surra, a kind of sleeping sickness similar to the well-known tropical disease of humans and caused by a trypanosome parasite which is carried by biting flies. It attacks camels in Africa and Asia and other animals including the horse, buffalo, elephant and tapir. Surra does not occur naturally in Europe. I searched for the manual but could not find it, indeed I never have found it again, but I had remembered enough to set out on a new trail. Surra produced lumps or bumps of some kind. I went to the Medical School library in Manchester to consult the books on protozoology. There it was. Surra: trypanosomiasis of camels. Caused by a rather elegant protozoan parasite in the blood. Common in Egypt, Africa, etc.

Could this be a case of tropical trypanosomiasis in darkest Manchester? I examined the camel once more and took more blood, this time to make smears which I could examine myself for the presence of the parasite. Not a thing. No parasite. More blood, more smears. Still nothing. I sat at the microscope with my eyes aching and my hopes of a clinching diagnosis receding. I decided to take more blood from the animal but at a different time of day, since some of these parasites are creatures of habit and only seem to go promenading in the blood at certain times of day. I took blood at night. Still nothing. Then I tried a sample first thing in the morning. The camel, miserable as it was, was becoming thoroughly fed up at the repeated jabs from my needle. I was having trouble washing the smell of camel puke from my hair. The latest sample was stained in the usual way with dyes to bring out contrasting colours in the blood corpuscles and anything else that might be there. I scanned field after field through the lenses until little red discs filled my eyes. Suddenly there it was! A beautiful object to look at, coloured by the stains at the moment of its death and preserved for ever, a sinuous twist of lilac and purple veil. A trypanosome. You only need one to clinch it. I had a case of surra.

When I rang up ICI and asked for what I needed the man at the other end of the telephone thought I was pulling his leg.

'You're D. C. Taylor of Rochdale and you've got a case of camel trypanosomiasis?' He paused. 'Rochdale in Lancashire, you mean?'

'Yes,' I said, 'and I believe you make a drug to cure it.'

The ICI man said he would have to have a word with somebody and I could faintly hear the comments as he left the telephone and recounted the gist of my request to the office at large. There was some guffawing and something about somebody having somebody else on. The man returned to the phone.

'Well, how many doses will you need? We only sell it for export normally. It's in packs of a hundred doses.'

'I only need enough to treat one camel,' I replied. 'Can you split the pack?' Rochdale doesn't see many camels. I imagined having difficulty getting rid of the other ninety-nine doses.

ICI turned out to be most co-operative. They sent me a specially packed single course of treatment for my surra case. The animal had obviously been infected with the parasite when it first came to Britain nearly three years previously. All that time the bug had been slowly nibbling away inside it. At least things turned out well: the anti-surra compound worked as efficiently in Manchester as it is said to do in Africa, the dropsy subsided and in due course the camel regained a plump, healthy weight.

Camels are fascinating animals, tough, uncomplaining about work and beautifully and functionally built, but the contents of their stomachs seem to have an affinity for suede leather. Once together the two cannot be parted. This I discovered when, clad in an expensive and much prized suede jacket but unprotected by an overall, I examined my first camel. I knew as we all do that camels spit but I did not realise what little it takes to make them spit. Camels will spit for the slightest

109

provocation, real or imagined, they will spit pre-emptively to start trouble or defensively even if only looked at in the wrong way. What is more, the word 'spit' conjures up a picture of relatively limited quantities of frothy saliva, the sort schoolboys eject, whereas camel spit is in fact a bottomless well of smelly, green, partly digested stomach contents that are sprayed as a broadside or aimed in a single noxious blob of flying soup. This makes examining camels something of a specialised art. Putting an old jacket over the camel's head is said to help but I have known a wily beast spit accurately down the sleeves of the garment.

Camels can also kick in any direction with any or all of their legs, if necessary at the same time, and they try to heighten the effect of spitting by making awful gurgling noises and extruding a heaving pink sausage, part of the lining of the mouth, from between yellow teeth. They can bite very severely and with purpose and Moses, a magnificent but stroppy male Bactrian camel at Manchester, is one of the most dangerous zoo animals I know. I saw what he did to a kindly old man who, without permission, went into the camel pen to stroke him. Camels can build up a pressure cooker of resentment towards human beings, then the lid suddenly blows off and they go berserk. In Asia when a camel gets to this high pitch of bottled-up tension the camel driver senses the brooding trouble and takes off his coat and gives it to the animal. Then, rather like the Japanese workers who are provided with special rooms where they can work off their frustrations and resentments by beating up models of their executives, the camel gives the garment hell. He jumps on it, rips it, bites it, tears it to pieces. When it is all over and the camel feels that it has blown its top enough, man and animal can live together in harmony again.

Andrew and I had ample opportunity to study the contrariness of the species at close quarters when we went twice in the same day from Manchester to Prague to pick up a consignment of Bactrian camels. The camels were from Asian Russia, semi-wild and grumpy. Some had vicious rope halters running tightly round their heads and through holes bored in their ears. They had been branded on the cheeks with hot irons months or years before and had been fitted with the halters when quite small. As the camels had grown the halters had cut deep into the flesh and in some places had disappeared completely beneath the skin. Before loading in Prague our first job was to cut off these evil devices but, even so, for one poor creature it was too late. The dirty rope sawing away interminably at its head had introduced tetanus germs into the body and it was showing the first symptoms of lockjaw, a terrible disease to witness. At least when we got it back to Manchester we were able to give it treatment and relieve the agonising muscular spasms, but the unfortunate animal died.

Everything went well with the loading at Prague. A communist soldier stood guard outside the aircraft's lavatory door to ensure that no-one stowed away in there, while the poor veterinary surgeon from Prague Zoo who handed the animals over to us was not even allowed to set foot inside the cargo hold or cabin at all. He would dearly have liked to see his charges settled down in the plane but the authorities were not taking any chances that he might somehow disappear amongst the grunting, shuffling crowd of Bactrians. Instead we gave him a bottle of whisky and some bottles of a superb new zoo animal anaesthetic and he gave us in exchange some Czech aerosols for treating skin diseases.

The camels behaved themselves perfectly. Once aboard the aircraft almost all of them sat quietly down and we did not need to use a single dose of sedative. The flight back to Manchester was uneventful, with not so much as a peep out of the animals. We landed at Ringway Airport where transport and lots of keepers from the zoo were waiting to help us unload. By this time all the camels were sitting down and relaxing. They were superb air travellers. Now we had to get them onto their feet to walk them down the ramp into the special fly-screened quarantine van that would take them to the zoo. Camels and their relatives, the llamas, alpacas and vicunas, are easily offended. They sit down for a variety of reasons such as annoyance, disgust, boredom, fright or just to be unco-operative. Sometimes, of course, they sit down for the pleasure of it. When sitting down they may insist on rising for the same reasons. The general rule is that they will do the exact opposite of what the humans round them want them to do. This was a typical case: the complete cargo of camels in the aircraft decided, as one camel, not to get to their feet. Presumably they felt that they had done us enough favours that day in allowing themselves to be loaded so easily and then transported across Europe and that it was time for them to give us a bit of stick.

We tried shouting, slapping, lifting tails, blowing down ears and prodding with a stick. Nothing worked. Camel spittle began to fly around. Not one solitary camel was prepared to budge. They sat quietly resting on their briskets as if bolted to the floor. In the end they won. Each one had to be lifted by hand and carried bodily down to the van. It breaks the backs of five or six men to pick up a mature camel in this way and we had fifteen on board and another fifteen in the second consignment waiting in Prague. At last it was done. We flew back to Czechoslovakia and collected the rest. Again they travelled perfectly but, once they had landed at Manchester, became completely unco-operative and had to be carried out like the first bunch. It made the sweating keepers curse when some strapping great bull, who had just insisted on being borne out like a pitiful stretcher case, stood up voluntarily when deposited in the quarantine van and projected a gurgling stream of stomach contents at his erstwhile bearers.

Once in quarantine in Manchester the camels had to be observed carefully for any sign of disease. As usual we found on the skin of several of them dry scaly areas where the hair had fallen out. They had mange, a very common complaint caused by a minute mite which burrows into the skin. That meant giving the camels special shampoos, spraying every square inch of their body surfaces with a stirrup pump. It is not easy to be sure that the animal is totally wetted by the shampoo but if it is not, a few mites may escape destruction and survive to spread rapidly over the body during the next few weeks. Ideally the camels should be made to swim through a deep dipping tank and their heads dunked under the surface briefly to ensure complete application of the anti-mange chemicals, but very few zoos have that facility.

Another problem Andrew and I found in the camels was the appearance in the droppings of a bacterium related to the tuberculosis germ. We arranged with Cambridge University to perform a delicate and accurate test on the droppings which would spot these germs, the cause of an illness named Johne's disease even when present in only minute numbers. Johne's disease, or paratuberculosis as it is sometimes called, can attack cattle, sheep and goats. Little is known about the effect of the germ on exotic ruminants, so when we began to find large numbers of the bacteria in some of the camels we became rather worried. The camels were not showing the typical symptom of chronic diarrhoea. Were they just carrying the germ harmlessly? Then after some weeks one of the animals began to lose weight and condition steadily. Despite intensive investigation and treatment it became a walking skeleton, but the only thing we could find were clusters of the Johne's bacterium in its droppings. Virtually nothing had been written about Johne's disease in species other than farm animals but we did stumble across a Russian scientific paper which said that the disease had been recorded in a substantial proportion of Bactrian camels and that it could cause death. Our camel in Manchester became in the end so weak and emaciated that it could no longer rise to its feet and the keepers had to bottle-feed it with gruel. One morning it was found dead. An autopsy found the wall of the intestine to be extensively damaged, and the microscope showed lying in the wall the little red rods that are Johne's bacteria.

So Johne's disease was able to treat camels with as little respect as it does domestic cattle. What was worse was that I soon spotted what looked like another case of the disease, this time in a rare sitatunga, a beautiful but very nervous antelope from the secluded swampy forests of Africa. Again there was no persistent diarrhoea as might have been expected but the other symptoms were highly suggestive and we found the germ lurking in the droppings. By now we were very alarmed. Through how many species could this tiny red rod that looks so insignificant under the microscope spread its havoc? No-one had ever seen a case of Johne's disease in sitatunga before. What other new ground were we doomed to break?

One major snag was that there was no certain cure for Johne's disease and vaccination was still being developed. We decided to try an experiment. The germ looks like and indeed is a close relative of the human tuberculosis bacterium. What if we did something not normally feasible for economic reasons in domestic cattle or sheep affected by Johne's disease and treated the sitatunga with a long course of drugs designed to combat TB in humans? We had no choice. Tragically, one of the sitatunga, a younster bred in the zoo, had died and we had found his bowels riddled with the complaint. The others must all go onto the treatment immediately.

Sitatunga panic violently for the slightest reason so handling them provides many headaches. Open the door into their paddock or startle them by some unusual noise after lights-out and they may dash frantically about, colliding with walls or fences and damaging themselves severely. The pop of the dartgun and the slap of the flying syringe are asking for trouble so to examine the sitatunga closely, except in urgent emergencies, I use crushed tranquilliser tablets mixed with their food. Like all antelopes and similar creatures, sitatunga require a far larger dose than a human being of twice the weight or more. To treat the sitatunga with daily doses of streptomycin or even twice-weekly shots of viomycin as used for TB was simply not practical. We would have to rely on rather more old-fashioned anti-tuberculosis chemicals mixed daily in the food.

The treatment seemed promising at first. Symptoms of the

disease faded, but although the numbers of bacteria in the droppings diminished it was impossible to eradicate them altogether and even after months of treatment the animals were not fully cured. The entrenched germs meant that recurrences were likely to occur – sadly, they did.

The finding of this disease in two zoo species prompted us to screen other likely candidates for possible unsuspected infection. More tests at Cambridge found it in a few other ruminants in the zoo. The management at Manchester, who always supported enthusiastically any health programme for the good of their stock, were keen to find out the extent of this hidden problem. In order to compare the position in Manchester with that elsewhere we obtained samples from animals in other British zoos. In a remarkable number of samples from a range of antelope, deer, gazelles and exotic cattle we found the germ.

Although all the zoos had been most willing to co-operate in supplying the samples, the reaction of a few zoos when we found evidence of Johne's disease was surprising. Ostrich-like, they stuck their heads in the sand. They were actually piqued that we had provided evidence that their stock had a potentially dangerous infection in its midst. There was nothing wrong with their stock, they protested. The whole things was absolute nonsense. It must have been some other harmless bug picked up from the grass and simply passed out through the intestines into the droppings! This latter possibility had been provided for in the test developed at Cambridge and we were certain that we were not dealing with cases of bacterial mistaken identity. Despite this, and although we had seen the bug chewing away at the bowel tissues of camels and sitatunga, some very respectable zoological collections dropped the whole matter like a hot potato. They could not contemplate the possibility that all was not well with the animals in their care. There is quite a grapevine in the zoo world and from time to time I hear of animals dying in some of the parks where we found positive samples. The post-mortem findings, so it is whispered, strongly suggest Johne's disease.

Twelve

What happens when a unicorn falls ill? You might suppose that along with mermaids, phoenixes, rocs and griffins these creatures are immune to earthly ills in their faery realms and come more within the province of the sorcerer or elf than the veterinary surgeon. Not so, for in the deserts of Arabia I have attended one of the rarest and most beautiful species on earth and the probable source of the fabulous unicorn.

The Arabian oryx is the most stunning in appearance of all the antelopes. A dazzling creamy colour, with crisp brown face and leg markings, tall and elegant, its head topped with a pair of long, tapering, backward pointing horns, it is superb. So symmetrically are the horns set on its head that viewed from the side it appears to have only one (unicorn) horn. Its colouring is perfectly suited to blend into a background of bleached and blazing sand. Similarly, its anatomy and physiology beneath the handsome exterior have evolved over the millennia into an amazing organism capable of living and reproducing in one of the world's most terrible deserts, the Empty Quarter of Arabia. With ingenious internal tricks to cope with the shortage of natural water and to stop its blood rising to boiling point in the searing heat, with finely tuned senses that can detect danger at great distances in shimmering air or locate springs of water under the sand, and with the ability to outrun all but the fastest carnivore, the Arabian oryx once prospered. Then came the hunters. It was a strong and brave collector of skin and horn who could penetrate the fastnesses of the oryx and at first, because of the risk and effort involved, the number of animals killed was not excessive. But when Arab sheiks with big air-conditioned Chevrolets and sub-machine guns took to updating the hunting, the death warrant for this wild, beautiful animal was sealed. They were slaughtered as trophies until it was believed that not one remained in the wild free state. At least the species did not become extinct, for one Arab sheik, Sheik Qassim of Qatar, captured a number of the oryx and set up a precious breeding herd on his desert farm. Another small herd was established at Phoenix Zoo, Arizona, and a programme started to reintroduce zoo-bred stock into the wild in Oman.

One grey, drizzly breakfast-time in November the telephone rang. It was the Director of Medical Services in Qatar, Dr Gotting. Sheik Qassim's oryx were dying like flies. Could I go at once to see what was up? A first-class ticket on the next flight to the Arabian Gulf would be waiting for me at London Airport.

My bag is always packed. As well as clothing, maps, notebooks and credit cards there are emergency drugs, a basic surgical kit, syringes and needles in sizes suitable for humming birds or hippopotamuses, bottles and plastic bags for samples and a complete range of anaesthetics. To save time on arrival the bag and its contents are just compact enough to be carried as hand baggage. While Shelagh checked that it was all in order I telephoned the Foreign Office: I would need to take the dart-gun which meant getting assistance in oiling the official wheels so that it could be carried out of the country with me. This weapon, designed to carry sleep and healing instead of death, fires an ingenious metal hypodermic syringe by means of carbon dioxide gas pressure. It is loaded with canisters containing carbon dioxide and can throw a syringe fast and accurately up to thirty yards or more. When the syringe hits the target it automatically injects the contents into the animal by means of a small explosive charge that powers the rubber plunger inside. I carry all types of needle in my bag, some suitable for the armour-plating of rhinoceros, some fine and slightly barbed for monkeys, and others with collars on them to ensure the right degree of penetration where under-skin

117

vaccination is required. I never use the crossbow, a powerful weapon which caused the death of a number of deer when I was a student. It throws the syringe with such force that there is a possibility of the whole thing, syringe, needle and flight, going in one side of an animal and out the other.

The dart-gun is a so-called prohibited weapon classed along with machine guns and the like, an odd arrangement for it is slow to load and no more lethal than the drug it is filled with, which may be penicillin or a vitamin solution. Nevertheless the authorities make a great fuss about it and insist on special Home Office licences as well as the usual firearms certificate. Taking the dart-gun overseas can mean days of form-filling and delay.

On this occasion, however, the Foreign Office Qatar Desk turned out to be most enthusiastic. There were political overtones to my visit, it seemed. The Qatar Government had their reasons for not wanting American assistance on the oryx problem and had asked the British for help. It was important that I handled the affair properly. After all, Sheik Qassim was the brother of the ruler of the tiny oil-rich state that juts out of Saudi Arabia into the waters of the Gulf. There would be no trouble over taking the gun and the embassy in Doha, the capital of Qatar, would smooth things for me at the other end. I was informed that the French were taking a lot of interest in Qatar and trying to extend their influence there. They had shown willing to involve themselves in the oryx problem too. The FO thought that it would be first-class if I could beat them to it, get to Doha first, sort the trouble out and generally fly the flag for British veterinary science!

Later that day I flew out to Doha and as night fell I had my first glimpses of Arabia, the bright flares at the oil well-heads flickering thousands of feet below in the darkness. When we landed at Doha in the early hours of the morning the scene on the tarmac was like something out of *The Seven Pillars of Wisdom*. Arabs in black robes and white turbans, carrying rifles and automatic machine guns and with bandoliers of gleaming bullets criss-crossing their chests, clustered round the bottom of the steps. At first I thought they were there for me, but then I saw that they were exchanging greetings with a small Arab gentleman in traditional dress who had preceded me down the gangway. Later I found out that he was the very man whose oryx I had come to examine, Sheik Qassim, and that the armed men were his personal bodyguard.

Dr Gotting, Dr Qayyum, whose was the Chief Veterinary Officer, and the Chief of Police made up my welcoming party, the latter having come specially to examine my dart-gun. With the minimum of formalities I was whisked through customs and immigration and taken to a hotel. I was impressed by the speed and efficiency; they certainly were not wasting any time. Over a cup of camomile tea I asked Dr Qayyum about the outbreak of disease in the oryx. I was anxious to begin work as soon as dawn broke and any history learned now would save valuable time.

'When was the last death, how many have died and do you have any fresh post-mortem material for me?' I asked.

Dr Qayyum looked a little embarrassed. 'Twelve animals died,' he replied, 'but I'm afraid we have no post-mortem material.'

'But when was the last death? Are any others likely to die in the next day or two?'

'The last death, Dr Taylor, was in April but on exactly which date in April I cannot recall.'

I was flabbergasted. It was now the middle of November and the last deaths in this apparent emergency had occurred in April, over six months before.

'But I believe you are having serious problems with the oryx,' I said after I had regained my composure. 'Are any ill at all at present?'

Qayyum shrugged his shoulders and made a despairing grimace. 'I am not sure,' he said, 'but His Excellency the Sheik is very worried about them. That is why he has returned today from London where he has been himself for treatment.

119

He is very, very fond of the animals. He says no more must die.'

'So you have no post-mortem reports or specimens from the last deaths?'

'Well, no. But we opened one or two.'

'What did you find in those, Dr Qayyum?'

'Nothing much; perhaps the lungs were redder than normal.'

'And you have no preserved specimens?'

He shook his head sadly.

'Well, how many oryx are left now?' I asked.

Dr Qayyum shrugged again. 'I do not know exactly, but tomorrow if you wish you can go to see them with my assistant, Dr Iftikhar. Then you can see exactly how many there are.'

At daybreak the following morning I set out from the hotel with Dr Iftikhar, a smartly dressed young Pakistani who had recently arrived in Qatar. Doha is a small town of dusty buildings set on the water's edge and backed by desert which rolls away into the vast Rub'al Khali, the Empty Quarter. Graceful dhows lie in the harbour side by side with modern steamships carrying fertiliser and chicken feed for the embryo livestock industry. There are opulent palaces surrounded by trees and elegant pierced walls, and a modern, cool, emerald-green mosque. Women in black veils, their faces hidden behind beaked black-gold masks, ride by in Lincoln Continentals and knots of men squat at street corners inspecting trussed hunting hawks. There are dim, bustling souks filled with the tinsmith's wares, vegetables, sherbet, spices and Kraft margarine. The dust swirls in the street as diggers and excavators work to build this new city out of the rocky desert. Nowhere can one escape the sound of Radio Cairo carried by the ubiquitous transistor radio.

We drove out into the desert, a flat khaki plain covered by rocks and rubble for as far as the eye could see. Small grey-green tufts of wiry shrubbery somehow survive in places and on these the nomadic shepherds graze their flocks of sheep and goats. On and on we travelled across the depressing flat land until a small oasis of trees came into view. As we got nearer I could see that a cluster of farm buildings and paddocks was set beneath the trees and nearby was a small unpretentious palace. This was Al Zubarrah, Sheik Qassim's weekend retreat, from where he keeps in touch with events in the capital by radio telephone. A tall radio antenna was fixed to the roof of the little mosque within the palace garden. A man sleeping on the ground in the shade of a windowless one-room hut by the gate of a large paddock awoke as we rumbled up and came forward to greet us. Dr Iftikhar introduced him as the man who looked after the oryx.

The paddocks were built on the desert sand with high walls of grey breeze blocks and wide wooden doors. It was imposs-ible to see what was inside them. Dense clouds of pigeons wheeled over the farm and the entire area was littered with rubbish and crusted with birds' droppings. Even so, I was excited. Within a few moments I would see for the first time the largest existing herd of an animal rarer than the giant panda or the komodo dragon. Few European zoologists had been to see Sheik Qassim's farm in the desert. The oryx keeper took us over to the paddock gate, struggled with a rusty lock and pushed open the heavy doors. We walked through into a sunlit compound which had a line of green trees planted all along one side.

Standing glowing in the morning sun at the far end of the paddock, all heads turned in our direction, were the oryx, about three dozen beautiful creatures of all sizes from calf to old bull, all motionless and alert with ears pricked and nostrils distended. This was *Oryx leucoryx*, the famed Arabian oryx. Quietly we walked towards them across the sand. There were troughs of sparkling fresh water, barley and some sort of rough salt supplement set out under the trees. Piles of lush, freshly cut lucerne lay on the ground nearby. The oryx certainly seemed to be fed and watered carefully. As we came within fifty yards of the herd they moved off, circling round us

121

close to the grey walls. What gorgeous creatures they were. Beige-coloured calves not yet grown into perfect proportion pressed between cantering adults with flanks of dazzling whiteness and horns as straight and even and shiny as rapiers. I had worked with other species of oryx such as the beisa and the scimitar-horned oryx, and my first short scientific paper published in my early days with zoo animals had concerned a fatal case of tapeworm cysts in a beisa oryx, but, handsome as these other species undoubtedly are, the Arabian oryx surely wins first prize in the oryx beauty contest.

There were thirty-three animals and all of them looked in tip-top condition, plump and well-rounded. Only one elderly female had a hygroma, a sac of fluid the size of a grapefruit (a sort of chronic housemaid's knee) on one knee joint.

'They look very well, Dr Iftikhar,' I said. 'Do they breed well?'

'We get six or eight calves each year,' he replied. 'The herd size increases quite rapidly, but then the disease seems to strike and we're down to around thirty again.'

Questioning him in detail about the last deaths in April produced little of importance. There was not much to go on, just the vaguest of histories. Whatever it was that was killing the oryx, it struck suddenly as a rapidly fatal epidemic and then apparently disappeared when the numbers of oryx had been trimmed back. This pattern suggested that overcrowding and population density might be important factors. But suppose one day the disease just went on spreading through the herd until it wiped out the lot or at least a minimum breeding group? It was a frightening thought. One minute the animals had appeared to be ill, dull and off their food and the next they were found dead: that would be consistent with anthrax, the deadly illness that crams the blood vessels with fast-multiplying, lethal bacteria. There must be millions of anthrax spores in the rubbish and offal lying around the farm.

While I stood and watched the oryx and they circled warily round us, there was a commotion in the air above us as a flock

122

of pigeons numbering about two thousand swept over the wall of the oryx paddock and descended on the troughs of barley. The oryx keeper chased them away and they rose in a noisy, dusty blue-black cloud.

'I've never seen so many pigeons in my life,' I remarked. 'Why does the Sheik keep so many?'

'To feed and train his falcons,' was the reply. 'After the oryx, Sheik Qassim's great love is to hunt the houbara.'

The houbara is a fast-flying species of bustard living in the desert. Rich Arab falconers will take fleets of air-conditioned cars, dozens of trained hawks and falcons and a retinue of staff into the Rub' al Khali for one or two weeks at a time and be perfectly satisfied if they return with just one houbara.

Dr Iftikhar showed me round the rest of the farm. As we went out of the gate of the oryx paddock a group of camels were ambling by. Their coats were sparse and the underlying skin was an unhealthy crusty pink. They were extensively affected by mange. Whenever they got the chance they would stop against the corner of a wall or the trunk of a tree and have a satisfying rub. Mange is common in camels and it makes them itch, but the rubbing helps to spread the disease. Dr Iftikhar explained that the camels were passing through the farm. The nomad herdsmen used the farm as a stopping place and every day one or two herds of camel or sheep would rest there, taking advantage of the water and shade for an hour or two while the herdsmen exchanged gossip and took a cup of tea with the Sheik's men.

We entered another paddock, but this one contained only seven minute Arabian gazelles which leaped about in panic as we opened the gate. Iftikhar explained that the Sheik had collected these also. Originally there had been nearly eighty but the disease had hit them, too. Again there were no post-mortem examination reports or preserved specimens. Another paddock contained sheep and goats, but what a difference from the oryx enclosure. The animals were thin and in poor condition. Their food troughs were empty. Many

123

had infected eyes, purulent noses and maggot-infested sores.

'These are a terribly poor lot, Dr Iftikhar,' I exclaimed, picking up a small, almost comatose lamb that lay dying in the fierce heat of midday. 'Riddled with disease and half-starved, I'd say.'

Dr Iftikhar began a verbose apologia. Yes, they were a problem. No, they didn't have enough food. Sadly, no-one seemed to be able to do anything about them. But it was all the fault of a batch of sheep brought in from Saudi Arabia. You really couldn't trust the people over there to eradicate their diseases, and so on. He rattled on and took me by the arm, drawing me away from the miserable flock that were unusually silent, so weak and debilitated had they become.

'I'm sure you don't want to get yourself messed up with these creatures, Dr Taylor.' He brushed flecks of wool and dirt from his natty suit. 'After all, you are here to see the oryx.'

'I'm here to look into the oryx disease problem,' I said, more than a little disgruntled. 'I may be six months late, but at least I may find out something by knowing what sort of sick animals the oryx have as their next-door neighbours. Please arrange for this lamb to be killed now so that I can do an autopsy on the spot.'

I could see in his face that I was disturbing the peace and order of Dr Iftikhar's routine. As for doing autopsies in the field – well! I could almost read his thoughts. Why couldn't this pernickety Englishman disappear into a hole in the ground?

'But we have no facilities, Dr Taylor. It is only a lamb. Lambs die all the time.'

'Of course they do, but they die from something. All I need I have in my bag. Please get me a container of water for my hands.'

When the skinny little body of the lamb was brought I crouched under the shade of a tree and made a crude dissection. It must have been the first post-mortem ever performed on a sheep at the farm. Dr Iftikhar stood some yards off, watching. The chest cavity was full of sticky, honey-coloured liquid. The tiny lungs were affected by dropsy and carried large areas of solid purple inflammation. The lymph glands draining the lungs were enlarged and angry-looking, spotted with bright scarlet haemorrhages. It looked like haemorrhagic septicaemia, a disease of cattle, buffalo, sheep and wild cud-chewing animals which is caused by a bacterium called Pasteurella. I took specimens for analysis and culture. If I could find Pasteurella in this lamb then perhaps I could begin to explain the sudden deaths in the oryx and gazelles. The teeming legions of foraging pigeons would be the obvious carriers of the disease over the wall to the oryx.

In the other farm buildings the earth floors were piled high with mounds of long dead birds, hens, turkey poults and pigeons. Emaciated hens stalked hungrily about, pecking at the remains of their fellows that were slowly rotting into the ground. Every room, cage, hut and pen contained dead or dying birds. Pigeons fluttered everywhere. Many of them were sick, their eyes half closed and the skin of the eyelids, at the corners of the mouth and around the nostrils distended with masses of warts and blisters. Pox virus was rampant. The decaying corpses of turkeys and hens bore the same ugly excrescences. I wondered what Andrew, who has a special interest in bird diseases and has published a paper on pox in falcons, would think of this charnel house. If Sheik Qassin was feeding pigeons to his valuable hunting birds, he must surely be suffering losses from pox attacks.

The farm was literally stuffed with diseased animals. Only the oryx and gazelles were in good condition and they alone showed any evidence of being systematically fed. Carrying samples of the oryx food including fresh and dried lucerne, I was driven back across the seventy miles of desert to Doha. Without dead or sick animals among the oryx there was little I could do to confirm the nature of the disease, but the sources of a hundred and one potentially lethal epidemics were easily identifiable. Haemorrhagic septicaemia was my favourite for the culprit.

On the way back to the city Dr Iftikhar asked me to give my opinion on a case of lameness in a horse at Ar Rayyan, the royal stables. We drove up to an imposing arrangement of white buildings. Round a vast sandy arena were rows of spacious, airy loose-boxes. It was most impressive. We stood in the sunlight as a groom led out a chestnut thoroughbred. It was thin and rangy and had a pronounced limp on one foreleg. I examined the leg and Dr Iftikhar described the history and his course of treatment. It was a case of navicular disease, inflammation of a peculiar but troublesome little bone that lies beneath the horny wall of a horse's (or zebra's) hoof. When we had agreed a plan for further therapy I remarked on the poor condition of the animal. Dr Iftikhar looked embarrassed once again.

'I'm afraid that the horses here have little food. There are sixty of them, blood horses from Britain, Ireland and Germany. But they belong to the ex-Emir.'

'What difference does that make?"

Dr Iftikhar puffed and scratched his head. 'Well, it's a peculiar business. The old Emir was deposed bloodlessly by the present ruler, his younger brother. Now he's in exile. But because its something of a family affair, all his belongings in Qatar remain his property. The new Emir and the rest of the family won't confiscate them, but on the other hand they won't find any money to maintain them. It doesn't matter very much in the case of buildings or motor cars, but unfortunately there are more serious consequences for his horses.'

'Do you mean that no-one feeds the horses?'

'Well, sometimes they get a little, but not often.'

'Why doesn't the Government sell or destroy the horses?'

'Because they belong to the exiled Emir.'

Iftikhar led the way into the well-equipped loose-boxes, in each of which was a horse. They were all obviously of first-quality breeding with fine heads and superb bones. There were greys and chestnuts, bays and blacks but every one was in some stage of plain, down to earth starvation. Some stood like hat racks, their fine skin pulled tight over their skeletons, others lay unable to rise. Some chewed at the sandy floor. Their droppings were a mixture of sand, wood dust and mucus. At least there was plenty of water but of any kind of food there was not a trace in the whole complex. I walked on past box after box, unable to believe my eyes. A stable full of animals that would be worth hundreds of thousands of pounds in Europe were being allowed to starve slowly to death. And I had been asked to look at a case of lameness!

'Doesn't all this eating of sand and earth produce gut trouble?' I asked, literally dizzy with disbelief. 'Surely you get colic cases galore?'

'Yes, we do. That's what finishes them usually. I treat them with pethidine if they're in pain.'

It may have been a bloodless deposing of the old Emir, I thought, but it had meant a cruel death for a collection of innocent animals brought far from the pastures of their birth.

'Is there nothing we can do about it?' I asked.

'I'm afraid not,' said Dr Iftikhar. 'It's very difficult to influence such matters. High politics, you know. Ruling family and so forth.'

I would try to do something about it.

Back in my hotel I decided to go for a swim in the sea before changing my clothes for one of Sheik Qassim's traditional audiences that evening. The waters of the Gulf behind the Alwaha Hotel were shallow, pale blue and highly inviting. As I swam I could see large dark shadows scurrying about on the ocean bottom but without goggles or a face mask I was unable to identify them. Then I saw an Arab wading about in the water, carrying a large tin slung round his shoulders and peering through the water with the aid of an empty jam jar. From time to time he would dive quickly beneath the surface and come up with the biggest pink and brown crabs I had ever seen. So that's what the scurrying shadows were. I swam on, thinking how delectable they would be when prepared in Shelagh's favourite way with the meat dressed with white wine, garlic and capers and roasted in the shell. Suddenly the Arab gave a mighty yell, dropped his tin and his jam jar and lunged off with great leaping strides towards the shore. I wondered if one of his quarry had laid hold of his foot, since the crabs were big enough to pinch severely.

Floating lazily on, I looked down through the clear water at the fuzzy shapes on the bottom and revelled in the cool caress of the sea. One of the dark shapes did not scurry like the others, in fact it was not on the sea bottom at all. It grew bigger. It was swimming towards me, effortlessly and straight as an arrow. It had the strangest head and it was brown on top and dirty white underneath. Suddenly I knew what had made the crab-catcher head so rapidly for dry land, for coming lazily towards me was a full-grown hammerhead shark. These fish, looking like one of the more far-fetched creations of a horror film studio, are definitely known to be man-eaters. The bizarre shape of the head, which is five times as wide as it is long, is unmistakable although its function is a mystery – perhaps these very strong swimmers use it as a sort of anterior rudder. Certainly they are not fussy about what they eat and I had seen them take dead dolphins caught in the nets in Florida. I felt very, very frightened.

On came the hammerhead. Even underwater I could see him now with less distortion. I did not dare turn away from him to swim towards shore, nor did I fancy the idea of standing on the bottom with the water up to my chest. Then, when he was about six feet away, another of the busily hurrying crabs, thank Heaven for a lowly crustacean, came teetering by. With its large, unblinking eyes the shark spotted the creature, and suddenly veered off diagonally downwards. Through the shimmering water I saw it smoothly pick up the crab in its jaws. Scrunch. The crab had disappeared. The hammerhead swirled round in the water, the tip of its tail flashed under my nose and in a moment it had gone, gliding calmly away into deeper water. I made my way to the beach. I did not swim in the Gulf again.

At six o'clock it was time to go to one of the Sheik's regular audiences held twice a day at his town palace or Majlis. At these audiences anyone, from the highest to the lowest in the community, has a chance to exchange a few words with or make a request of the Sheik. With Dr Gotting I drove into the Majlis through an archway guarded by the armed men I had seen at the airport. Inside there were cool courtyards with fountains and orange trees, and cloisters where patient hawks sat hooded on their blocks. We removed our shoes and entered a brightly lit room decorated with the heads of Arabian oryx mounted as trophies. At the far end on a decorated chair sat the Sheik and around him were seated members of the aristocracy and Government ministers. The chair on his immediate right was empty. Here for short periods would sit those with whom he wished to talk or who had a petition to make. Down the sides of the room sat all sorts of other people, the least important and most shabbily dressed next to the door. As we entered the Sheik rose to greet us. The rest of the people in the room also stood. We walked the length of the room, shook hands and retired to two seats halfway along the wall. Everyone took their seats once more. A little whispering was going on and the Sheik would occasionally beckon to some member of his staff who would come to sit briefly at the Sheik's right and talk in low tones. A servant circulated continually with a tray of small handleless cups and an ornate gold pot full of camomile tea. My cup was kept permanently brimming, and I had to learn to shake the empty cup from left to right to indicate that I did not want any more of the rather insipid beverage.

It was a very leisurely business. Shabbily dressed peasants from near the door would seize their chance to sit in the vacant chair and then quickly murmur their request into the Sheik's ear. Rarely was anyone there for more than a minute or two. If the Sheik decided that action had to be taken, he would beckon to an official and give his instructions. Dr Gotting explained that it was at just such an audience that Sheik Qassim had suddenly become alarmed about the condition of the oryx and had commanded him to get professional help from Britain immediately. Although the good Doctor supervised the running of the hospitals and was in no way involved with the veterinary services, he had had to take it in hand. The order might equally well have been given to the Chief of Police or the Director of Oil Production. No matter who is given the order, he has to execute it.

After half an hour and an overabundance of tea Dr Gotting went to the chair and spoke with the Sheik. When he returned he whispered to me that the Sheik had asked him whether I had brought my family with me yet. Apparently he expected me to stay permanently!

'He thinks you are here for good to look after his oryx. He wasn't very pleased when I said you were only here on a short visit. He thinks you should remain ad infinitum.'

Much as the Arabian oryx fascinated me I could not conceive a worse fate than to spend all one's days out on that awful farm in the desert. A few minutes later the chair beside the Sheik was empty again.

'Right, off you go now,' whispered Dr Gotting.

I went across to the chair and sat down. An interpreter came to stand behind the Sheik.

'His Excellency asks what you think of the oryx at Al Zubarrah,' he said.

I realised I would have to get my points over quickly and I wanted also to raise the matter of the horses starving at Ar Rayyan.

'The oryx are very fine,' I began, 'but the cause of the disease cannot be precisely established yet. However I do recommend splitting the herd into two, separating and . . .'

Abruptly the Sheik stood up. Everyone else followed suit as usual. A close member of the Sheik's family, a nobleman in fine robes lined with gold, had entered. Dr Gotting beckoned to me to return to my place. The nobleman kissed his kinsman the Sheik and sat down in the seat that I had vacated.

130

'That's it for today,' murmured my companion.

'What? Do you mean my interview is finished?' I replied.

'Yes, that is his first son and there are a couple of imams, religious leaders from Cairo, waiting to come in. You've had your chance for today. We might as well leave.'

We slipped out of the room. Although I stayed for another seven days taking samples from the oryx and the farm for analysis in England, and although I attended several more audiences, I never got another chance to plonk myself down in the vacant chair. I was always beaten to it.

Although I had not been able to deal with any cases of actual disease in the oryx I was able to suggest measures for tackling the next outbreak and, most important, for getting me the material required for diagnosis. I wrote a long report detailing my ideas for cutting out the spread of disease and improving health generally at the farm, and I wrote scathingly about the horses in the royal stables. Copies were sent to the Sheik and various Government bodies. Then, loaded with samples of oryx droppings, lucerne, hay, blood, barley, and various other possibly useful substances, I returned to England. The customs officer at Manchester Airport extracted the plastic bag containing half a pound of dried lucerne from my luggage, opened it and sniffed suspiciously.

'Bringing rabbit food all the way from the Persian Gulf then, eh?' he said, crumbling some of the leaves between his fingers and sniffing some more. 'Doing some long-distance hay-making?'

'It's not cannabis.' I told him, and showed him my collection of droppings and blood. He believed me.

It was the same customs officer who inspected my bags two years later and grimly withdrew a bag containing five pounds of uncooked foreign meat.

'It's the placenta of a dolphin that aborted in Majorca. I'm taking it to Professor Harrison of Cambridge as a gift,' I explained on that occasion.

'Oh yes,' said the customs officer, recognition dawning on

his face, 'you're the bloke who usually has a bag full of antelope crap!'

After my first visit to Qatar I kept in contact with Dr Qayyum and his team and sent out drugs and sample bottles ready for the next outbreak of disease in the oryx. Analysis of the food, blood and droppings had not brought up anything abnormal, but I had had a telephone call from a foreign animal dealer who had heard of my visit to the Middle East.

'I've got a proposition for you,' he said. 'I must get hold of at least three Arabian oryx. If you can persuade the Qataris to part with them, I'll give you £2000.'

'What exactly do you want them for?' I asked.

'You can explain to the Qataris that they are to introduce new blood into the American herd. They'll perhaps part with them if they think it will be good for conservation of the species. Then I'll ship the three to the States and exchange them for an identical threesome which I'll send somewhere else.'

It seemed rather tortuous. 'Exactly where else?' I asked.

The dealer was reluctant to say but I pressed him, knowing that I was his best hope of obtaining such exceptionally rare stock. Eventually he said, 'Actually to Israel. The Israelis are building up a collection of all the animals that existed in the original Palestine. The Arabian oryx is one of them and you can imagine their chances of getting them from the Arabs.'

Not wishing even to dip my toe into the treacherous waters of Middle Eastern politics, I politely told the dealer what to do with his proposition.

It was exactly a year later that the next urgent call came from Qatar. This time there had not been the same inexplicable delay in seeking help, but three days had still elapsed before I was requested to fly out without delay. Six oryx had died and, although no bodies were available for my inspection, tissue specimens and bacterial swabs had been taken. At the farm out in the desert nothing had changed. The clouds of pigeons still filled the sky above the paddocks. Camels and goats wandered at will through the farm and the sheep were in an even more desperate state than before. Again the remaining oryx seemed healthy and in good condition. I examined the bits of lung and other organs that Dr Qayyum and Dr Iftikhar had taken from the dead oryx. It looked like a haemmorhagic septicaemia. I sent portions by air to England and had others processed at the local hospital laboratory.

There were many sick sheep on the farm. Each day there was a pile of new carcasses outside the paddock gates. I walked among the flocks with my stethoscope and listened to the chests of sick and dying animals. The fluid noises and harsh roaring of pneumonia were always to be found. I asked Dr Iftikhar again about the innumerable pigeons.

'Why can't we cut down the numbers of those birds?' I demanded.

'The Sheik will not do it,' he replied. 'He says they are essential for the falcons.'

The results came back by telex from the English laboratory. It was haemmorhagic septicaemia in the oryx and the swabs taken from their tissues had grown pure cultures of Pasteurella bacteria. I was finding the same germ in all the poor sheep that died at the farm, their lungs studded with angry red areas of pneumonia. At least drugs existed to combat the disease.

'I am going to begin a vaccination programme for the oryx,' I told Dr Iftikhar, 'and I'm going to give serum and vaccine to every sheep and goat on the farm.'

The Pakistani looked dismayed. 'It will be necessary first to request permission from His Excellency the Sheik,' he said. 'Without permission, which is difficult to obtain, we cannot inject the oryx; he loves them so much.'

'It will have to be done,' I insisted. 'I'll go to the Majlis to have audience with him tonight.'

It was the fear of injections which had led to the foolhardy practice at the farm of mixing broad-spectrum antibiotics with the food for the oryx. This sounds like a simple way of administering anti-bacterial drugs to nervous or dangerous

133

wild animals, but in a cud-chewing animal the antibiotics kill most of the harmless bacteria in its stomach which are essential for its special type of digestion. The consequences can be serious and often fatal. I wondered whether any of the deaths at Al Zubarrah had been due more to the therapy than to the complaint.

'And unless we do the sheep and goats as well there's not much point,' I carried on. 'Think of the improvement in their value as well.'

'But vaccinating sheep!' exclaimed Dr Iftikhar. 'There are so many!'

'We are going to do it, you and me,' I replied firmly. He looked very miserable.

I went to the evening audience alone and eventually bagged the vacant chair beside the Sheik. Through the interpreter I explained: 'I can help your oryx, Your Excellency, but I need to vaccinate all of them and all the sheep and goats. And to do the oryx I would like to have a strong wooden cattle crush built.'

For a few seconds the Sheik pondered and sipped his tea, then he said a few words to the interpreter.

'The interview is over,' he said. 'His Excellency says you can have what you want. There will be forty men at the farm tomorrow morning to build whatever structure you require. And you can do all the sheep and goats.'

The following day, fortified and refreshed by a pile of water-melons, the forty labourers and I built an elaborate tapering cattle crush against one wall of the oryx paddock. At the end of the crush was a trap designed to hold an individual animal while I vaccinated it. Carpenters cut wood to size, some men dug holes for posts and others unrolled heavy-gauge wire mesh and nailed it to the posts. By midday we were ready to try it out. We carefully drove the herd of oryx into the wide mouth of the crush. As they were pressed in slowly towards the narrow neck they suddenly panicked. In unison they launched themselves at the sides of the crush. As if it were made of paper the whole contraption fell flat before the charging animals. Ten seconds later not a single piece was left standing.

Unharmed and impassive, the oryx gathered in a distant corner of the paddock and surveyed the scene of our fruitless labours. I would have to use the dart-gun. I loaded every syringe I had with a dose of the vaccine and applied a blob of antibiotic jelly to the needle tips. Although the darts were sterile, as they entered the animals' skins they might take in a particle of soil or dust adhering to the hair, and I was not prepared to run the slightest risk of losing any animals from tetanus. When all was prepared I sent everyone including the vets away so that I could move about the oryx paddock quietly and alone, picking off one animal at a time with the minimum disturbance or fuss. That way I could avoid shooting at moving targets. This was important because in each case I wanted to place a subcutaneous injection precisely over the ribs just behind the shoulder. Any reaction to the vaccine in that place would not interfere with movement and would soon disperse. In order not to inject the vaccine too deep I had selected needles only half an inch long which carried fat little collars to control the depth of penetration. One by one I darted the oryx, who were not disturbed by the relatively quiet gas-powered gun. After delivering its contents each syringe fell out of the animal onto the sand and I retrieved it. It was all over in an hour and a half. Within ten days the oryx would be carrying a good level of protective antibodies in their bloodstreams.

I arranged with Dr Iftikhar for him to repeat the process in two to four weeks, then set off to see about vaccinating the sheep and goats by hand.

'Surely we can leave the vaccination of these animals to the farm men,' said Iftikhar. 'I'm sure you don't want to go in with all those hundreds of smelly creatures.'

'I want to see every animal properly vaccinated and dosed with antiserum this afternoon,' I replied. 'I'll do half and you do the others.'

'But the men don't really want to catch the sheep.' Iftikhar was looking positively awkward.

'All right then,' I said, 'I'll catch them and do them myself.'

I went into the sheep paddock with a multidose syringe, grabbed a sheep, vaccinated it and bundled it out of the gate to the watching group of men and Dr Iftikhar. I did another and another. Still the men watched. It was going to take a long time at this rate to do all the hundreds of sheep but I was determined that all susceptible animals were going to be done. Eventually the shamefaced knot of men at the gateway came reluctantly in dribs and drabs into the paddock and began catching animals. Dr Iftikhar filled his syringe and before long we were whistling through the flock at a fine old rate.

Before leaving for England I walked round the whole of the farm again. The pox-infested birds were still everywhere, both dead and alive. Out in the small irrigated fields where the lucerne for the oryx was grown I walked down the rows of succulent green plants and noticed many plastic bags, some containing quantities of white powder, lying on the soil. The bags bore bold skull and crossbones symbols in bright red. The white powder was an insecticide containing the extremely dangerous organo-phosphorus type of chemical. The farm workers had used the stuff and then idly dropped the seemingly empty bags as soon as they had finished with them. In places the white powder was actually caked onto the leaves of the lucerne plants. It worried me. This stuff was fine when properly diluted with water and sprayed, but what if the oryx were fed lucerne contaminated with the neat, concentrated powder? I pointed out the risk to Dr Iftikhar and he had words with the labourer in charge of the fields. There was no risk, said the labourer, as they were not going to crop that area for quite a while. He would see that the bags were gathered up and that the powder was washed off the leaves in future. One month later I received a letter from Dr Qayyum requesting advice on treating animals posioned with organo-phosphorus insecti-

136

cides. Three oryx had eaten lucerne contaminated with the chemical and had developed the typical symptoms of poisoning affecting the nervous system. One of the animals had died by the time he wrote the letter and the other two were gravely ill. Unfortunately the letter took two weeks to reach England and although I immediately cabled detailed advice, once again I was far too late.

Something else once arrived from Qatar. I went down to breakfast to find a small parcel covered with Qatari stamps waiting on the dining table. I opened it and out fell a brain! Stuck to the noisome object was a stained piece of notepaper. After hurriedly removing the thing and all its wrappings to my office I scrubbed my hands with iodine soap and pulled on a pair of plastic gloves. Then I read the letter, which was from Dr Qayyum. The brain was from a dog with suspected rabies and would I kindly confirm or deny please!

With all the careful rules and regulations, quarantine provisions and the lot designed to keep the British Isles free from the horrific scourge of rabies, here was a mass of putrefying material possibly loaded with active rabies virus arriving as calmly as could be on my breakfast table after wending its way through the channels of the Post Office. I telephoned the Ministry of Agriculture immediately. They seemed puzzled as to the correct thing to do.

'None of the rules fit,' said one of the Ministry men to whom I spoke.

'It's not from a British dog so an investigation isn't called for,' offered another.

'You haven't asked for its importation so you can't be held responsible for not getting a licence,' a third reassured me.

'You can't quarantine a rotting brain,' said a fourth, plaintively.

In the end they left it to me to deal with. I was dumbfounded. Nobody in the Ministry seemed to care that I might be about to put Rochdale on the map as the place where rabies entered Britain, possibly never again to be eradicated. I took the brain and all the packing paper, put them in a box filled with carbolic acid and then incinerated the whole thing. If rabies was indeed in that brain, not a virus particle escaped.

Thirteen

On my way home from my first visit to Qatar I made a detour via a zoo at Marseilles in the South of France. The morning after my arrival, M. Villemin, the owner of the zoo, telephoned my hotel to say that he was sending a vehicle and chauffeur to pick me up. After breakfast I went out of the foyer of the hotel onto the busy street. There was M. Villemin in his car, but parked directly in front of the hotel steps was a motor cycle and, waiting patiently on the driving seat dressed in sweater, trousers and peaked cap, was a large and unconcerned-looking chimpanzee.

'Get on the pillion seat behind Henri,' M. Villemin shouted from the car when I appeared. 'He is a good driver.'

The centre of Marseilles is hardly a sleepy Provençal hamlet and the zoo was about a mile or more away. I consider myself a reasonably competent driver in most European countries but the higher mysteries of the logic behind French driving habits continue to elude me. I would not lightly venture out behind the wheel of a tank into that nine o'clock maelstrom of furiously honking Citroëns and wobbling bicycles. But a chimpanzee!

'But does he know the way?' I asked nervously, stalling.

'Of course he does, you can rely on Henri,' was the reply.

The hotel commissionaire came over and reassured me. 'Don't worry, Monsieur,' he said. ' 'E 'as been 'ere to collect guests before.'

I did not dare ask whether all the previous guests were alive and well and living in sanatoria. Instead I walked up to the motor cycle. The chimpanzee looked at me blandly, raised himself and kicked the starter. Brrrm-brrrm, brrrm-brrrm: he revved the engine expertly with one hairy black hand and picked his nose slowly with the other. Brrrrrm-brrrrrm. I put my leg over the machine and sat down on the pillion seat tentatively, keeping some of my weight on my feet and ready to auto-eject at the first sign of disaster. Henri now looked straight ahead. He revved again, short crackling bursts of the two-stroke engine. I put my arms round the muscular waist of my driver and stuck my thumbs firmly into the top of his trousers.

I think it was at this stage that I began to perspire.

Henri looked to his right, stopped picking his nose, revved more strongly and then, when he saw a gap in the traffic, kicked in the gear with a practised bare foot and slipped away from the kerb in a tight turn.

'Put your feet up, M. Taylor,' I heard M. Villemin call as he pulled out behind us into the road.

I lifted my feet onto the rests and found to my delight that we were cruising in a straight line at about fifteen miles an hour straight up the boulevard. It was perfect Highway Code stuff. Unlike the drivers of several of the vehicles on either side of us, Henri knew where he was going and how to go about it. We approached a red light. I tensed. I was definitely perspiring now. The cross-traffic was in full spate. Was it really true that chimpanzees were colour blind? This seemed a novel way of proving the point. Henri slowed down and, like the good motor cyclist he was, maintained our balance at very slow speed by weaving slowly from side to side hoping to maintain some momentum until the lights changed. They did. Brrrrm-brooom-brooooom. Henri took us smartly away with a flick of the wrist and an effortless change of gear.

The next obstacle was a traffic policeman. No problem. As Henri and I approached, the officer smiled, held up the cross-flow and waved us on. Henri crackled past him without so much as a nod or a 'bonjour'. We were getting close to the zoo but would now have to negotiate some narrow streets with several sharp corners. At the end of the boulevard we came to the first turn. Hunched over the handlebars Henri leaned beautifully into the bend. Less accustomed to motor bikes and without the chimpanzee's perfect sense of balance, I rocked awkwardly on my seat and clutched Henri's tummy. The machine wobbled. Uncomplainingly Henri corrected the wobble. I did not dare look round to see if M. Villemin was still following. Henri stared fixedly ahead and I crouched uncomfortably behind the purposefully hunched body. Henri took us nippily along the street, overtook a man pushing a handcart, swerved into the gutter to avoid a dog lying in the middle of the road and then got us back on course by a smart twist of the handlebars. Two more corners, down a hill fast enough to make Henri's saucer-shaped ears flip back and, with a turn into which he leaned over with what seemed to me more than a little flashiness, we arrived in the zoo drive. Henri cut the revs back and we tootled through the grounds to the ape house. Henri braked and brought the bike to a halt. He stood supporting it with his feet while the engine ticked over. I dismounted and walked round to face my driver, who looked at me unblinkingly and began to pick his nose again. It was all in a day's work for a chimp. Just a routine pick-up, nothing to get excited about.

Although M. Villemin had trained Henri to such a degree that he could cope with the murderous Marseilles traffic as well as any human driver and better than most French ones, handling the great apes generally calls for patience, cunning, skill and plain good luck. The discovery of effective tranquillisers for primates at least avoided the unpleasant use of nets and catching bags. As well as panicking the animal these methods of handling were dangerous for the humans involved. I myself was badly bitten by an ape incarcerated securely in a bag made of sacking because although I could not tell which bit of him was which wriggling and protesting under the opaque material, he could glimpse my fingers through the weave of the hessian and sank his canine teeth into them.

Nor were the old methods of control reliable. Most chimpanzees could be conned by waving a plastic snake at them but some, instead of retreating in apprehension, would advance boldly. One keeper tried waving a plastic reptile at a rebellious chimp who had broken into a food store. Not in the slightest taken in, the ape jumped forwards, grabbed the keeper's thumb, spun round and wrenched it off at the root as clean as a whistle. Some keepers of great apes would rely on chemical warfare in times of emergency and squirt ammonia at their unruly charges from plastic lemons which they always carried in their pockets. That was all very well until one was faced by a determined orang-utan. These gentle and most amiable apes would, if roused, do battle unconcernedly when wreathed in choking clouds of ammonia fumes. They seemed oblivious to the irritant and obnoxious chemical and neither coughed nor sneezed nor streamed with tears.

The introduction of phencyclidine and ketamine anaesthetics brought about dramatic changes in the handling of great apes. The drugs could be darted into an ape painlessly or given in a fruit drink. Even so, it is unwise to let a primate see you slipping a Mickey Finn into its favourite tipple. When I first began, several drinks which I had spiked in full view of a curious and wily chimp or gorilla were either thrown back at me or tipped tidily down the nearest drain. No other group of animals is as good as they are at detecting that sort of medical skulduggery!

One morning not long after I had qualified I was called urgently to Manchester Zoo. Adam, the male orang-utan, had escaped from the great ape house. It was the height of summer and Adam had gone to visit the Miniland, an exhibition of miniature fairy-tale villages and model tableaux from children's stories. When I arrived Adam was sitting on the partly demolished cathedral of Nôtre Dame chewing the leg off the hunchback. He gazed at us blandly as he chewed. I approached him slowly, accompanied by Len, his keeper. Len talked soothingly to him: he had looked after the orang since it was the size of a cat. How were we to get Adam back into his quarters? I had phencyclidine in my bag but at that time no dart-gun. Having the dope was fine but how was I going to be able to administer it? Adam threw the mutilated torso of the hunchback at us and grimaced threateningly. He shuffled truculently off, pausing only to pick up one of the three bears and to knock down Don Quixote's windmill with it. Adam made for the open spaces of the zoo gardens. Off to see some action among the crowds, he did not even glance back at us as he lolloped smoothly over the ground. Len, Matt Kelly, the zoo director and I followed anxiously. A mature orang-utan is immensely powerful, as Len had reason to know – an orang had recently sunk its teeth through one of his shoes and bitten off one of his toes. Adam might cause panic among the visitors. He had the muscular power of three full-grown men: what if he grabbed hold of a child?

Fortunately Adam, like most orang-utans, was a shy and undemonstrative creature without the brash exhibitionism of the chimpanzee or the mercurial changes in mood of the gorilla. As he wandered across the flower beds, now trailing an umbrella 'borrowed' firmly but without physical violence from an astounded passer-by, he spied a small wooden hut used by the gardeners. He went in and started to vandalise the interior. At least he was confined. We crept up to the door and bolted it. Adam was too busy smashing plant pots to notice us. What now? How to move the orang from A to B was the problem.

We sat outside and waited and discussed the matter. Len looked at his watch.

'It's almost eleven o'clock,' he said. 'It's his soup time!'

When I had taken over the care of the animals at Manchester Zoo I had introduced the feeding of plenty of meat to the great apes. Best pig's liver, chicken and mincemeat were given daily. Animal protein of this kind is essential for the apes' complete health and indeed it has produced a remarkable increase in the length and glossiness of their coats. All the meat is cooked to avoid risk of infection and the left-over gravy with added vegetables, herbs and cereals, is made into a soup which is given to the animals at eleven o'clock as a mid-morning pick-me-up. The apes seem to appreciate it greatly.

'Can you put some dope in the soup?' Len went on. 'He'll probably take it.'

It was a good idea. Len went off to fetch the warm broth while I measured out a dose of phencyclidine with a syringe. Adam's bright orange eyes watched us through the hut's small window. When Len returned I took the mug of soup and went round to the windowless rear of the hut, away from those orange eyes, and mixed in the sedative. I went back and gave the mug to Len. Adam was now sitting on a pile of shattered plant pots by the window. His stomach told him it was time for elevenses. Len pushed the window open and passed the mug through. Most politely Adam took his soup and drank it, smacking his lips and licking the mug dry as far as his tongue could reach. We watched and waited. Slowly but surely Adam's upper eyelids became heavy. He began to drool a thin thread of saliva and his lower lip sagged. In ten minutes he was asleep and then we carried him, like some pot-bellied and surfeited potentate, back to his house.

Adam and I still meet professionally from time to time. He never produced any offspring during his years at Manchester and the blame was put on him since we could find nothing wrong with any of his wives. Similarly Harold, the male orang at Flamingo Park Zoo, had not been blessed with heirs. We decided to swap Adam for Harold to see if an exchange of mates would remedy the situation. By this time I had a dart-gun and decided to dart Adam, drive him over to Flamingo Park, do the same to Harold and carry him back to Manchester. The orangs could sit beside me in my car.

On the day of the exchange I loaded a couple of syringes with phencyclidine and carefully greased the needle points with penicillin cream to deal with any germs that might be lurking on the dusty skin. Adam was soon lightly anaesthetised and we carried him to my car and sat him on the front seat. The safety belt kept him nicely in position. I set off, with Adam sitting stupefied next to me. He was in a sort of twilight world and with any luck would not start coming round for a couple of hours, long enough for me to make Flamingo Park – just. To be on the safe side I put a loaded syringe containing another dose of phencyclidine on the shelf below the dashboard. This is a wise precaution and I have once or twice managed to stick an injection into the ham muscle of an ape while bowling along the motorway and holding the wheel with one hand. Such irresponsible driving cannot be recommended but is essential when the anthropoid co-driver rouses quicker than anticipated and reaches for the gear lever as a support or tries to pick his ear with the trafficator control.

I reached Flamingo Park uneventfully with the dreaming Adam. He was still too doped when we put him into the orang house with his two new wives to appreciate the touching way they brought presents of lettuce to their lord and master. When Adam was safely installed I darted Harold, he was carried to my car and without further delay I set off back to Manchester. It was a hot day and Harold turned out to be a trifle flatulent. It became very necessary to wind down the windows. The orang sat comfortably behind the safety belt, his legs dangling over the edge of the seat and his arms in his lap. By the time I reached Leeds it was obvious that Harold's liver was a much more efficient destroyer of phencyclidine than Adam's and that the drug was rapidly being broken down by his system. The first signs were when Harold slowly stuck his arm out of the window and began to clench and unclench his leathery hand in the typical manner of an ape under light phencyclidine anaesthesia. A glance told me that I would have to top him up with a bit more dope in order to reach Manchester, and I decided to stop and attend to him as soon as I had cleared the busy traffic of Leeds city centre. Harold fidgeted slightly in his seat and began slowly to lick his lips. His other hand was now creeping slowly, ever so slowly, around the base of the gear stick. Still barely conscious of what he was doing, Harold drooled while the strong thick fingers of his right hand unpicked a piece of plastic trim with a loud crack. The index finger of the hand, moving as if with a mind of its own, entered the hole it had made and gained purchase on a bigger piece of plastic. Crack! At this rate I would be driving on a naked chassis by the time I reached Huddersfield. There were red traffic lights ahead. As soon as I got through them I would pull up and give him the knockout drops.

I stopped at the lights in the middle of three lanes of traffic. On my near side stood a paper boy on a bicycle, his canvas bag of newspapers slung over his shoulder. He was too busy watching for the green light to notice the fat, red-haired drunk sitting in a car by his elbow. The light changed and I let out the clutch, my eye fixed on a place a couple of hundred yards ahead where I might park briefly. Suddenly there was a piercing yell. I looked in my mirror. Nothing to see. 'Oooooow! Heeeeeey!' There was the cry again, somewhere to my left and behind me. I slowed down and looked over the head of Harold. Stuck like a fly to the outside of my car was the paper boy. His bicycle was lying some yards behind in the middle of the road. But what was the adhesive that made him cling so closely to the vehicle's side? Then I saw that Harold's wandering left hand had come across the boy's canvas bag when we were stopped at the lights. As soon as we moved off the hand had tightened powerfully by reflex action round the canvas sling of the bag and the lad had been dragged off his bike like a stone from a catapult. I stopped and went round to release Harold's catch. Fortunately the boy was not injured. I retrieved his bicycle, introduced him to the sleeping ape and let him hold my bottle while I prepared more dope. The lad soon recovered his wits and I rather fancy that being unhorsed by an orang-utan made his day. I still wonder whether anyone believed him when he went home and related how, like something out of a crazy gangster film, a car had pulled up alongside him in the middle of Leeds and a fat ugly orang-utan had tried to kidnap him.

If there is one habit which orang-utans have mastered it is

spitting. I have several orang friends who could make those tobacco-chewing expectorators in Western films look positive beginners in the accuracy stakes. Harold, now at Manchester, is pretty good at hitting small targets up to ten feet away but the champion is a male orang at Rhenen Zoo in Holland. He spits with real style both standing upright or when hanging upside down. Indeed I swear he can spit inswingers, so adept is he at reaching intended victims even if they stand behind someone else. Intended victims include veterinary surgeons who have given him medicals and subjected him to similar indignities in the past.

For underhand spitting Jo-Jo, the gorilla at Manchester, held the prize. What he lacked in accuracy he made up for in sneakiness. Jo-Jo's centrally heated, stainless steel fitted quarters had heavy metal doors. It was through a small spyhole in one of these doors that I poked my dart-pistol when gunning for Jo-Jo to anaesthetise him. For several years Jo-Jo had what we felt fairly conclusively was migraine. I closely examined every part of him, taking X-rays, electro-encephalograms and so on, to pinpoint the cause of recurrent bouts of severe headache which he suffered. Of course, all the medical examinations meant dartings, since you cannot handle a 400-pound male gorilla any other way. So Jo-Jo knew that the spyhole in the door was something of a nuisance. The typical procedure went like this.

First I put my eye to the hole to see where Jo-Jo was. I then loaded the dart-pistol while Jo-Jo looked through the hole at me. I could just see one dark shining eye. I returned to the hole to see where Jo-Jo was positioned now and wham! A ball of spittle zipped through the hole and hit me in the eye. Having wiped my face I poked the gun through the hole and squinted down the barrel. There was just enough room for me to see what I was aiming at. No gorilla – Jo-Jo was crouching close to the door below my line of sight. Now he grabbed the metal barrel of the pistol. He could not haul the whole weapon through the small hole, but he had a good try. His next move

147

was to spike my gun before I could get a bead on him. He popped up, opened his mouth and spat long and hard up the barrel of my gun. I withdrew the pistol for on-the-spot de-spitting and Jo-Jo moved back to the hole. As I busied myself cleaning the barrel I felt a blob of warm, sticky saliva hit the back of my neck. First rounds always went to Jo-Jo.

Jo-Jo and his mate, Suzy, first arrived in Manchester as young babies. Gorilla infants are notoriously delicate and easily succumb to germs brought in by human beings. We took every precaution to give them a strong and healthy start, including a ban on any of the great apes being taken out of the zoo to children's parties, fêtes and the like. That cut out the major source of 'flu, colds and infantile ailments. Using glass walls instead of bars for the heated indoor compartments in an ape house also plays a significant part in preventing the spread of bacteria and viruses from the public to the animals. All the keeping staff were regularly vaccinated against influenza and screened for tuberculosis. Tuberculosis still crops up from time to time in the apes and monkeys in zoos that I visit. It is a disease that does not occur in the wild primate but which can cause rapid death once the animals come into contact with man. It is a much more lethal disease in apes and monkeys than in man and if left untreated always results in death. A typical tragedy had occurred shortly before the baby gorillas' arrival when I had had the agonising job of destroying three chimpanzee friends of mine and a pair of gorgeous and valuable silver-leaf langur monkeys which were literally riddled with tuberculosis. We discovered that they had caught it from a keeper who was spreading the germs although not feeling ill himself.

Jo-Jo and Suzy were not going to suffer that kind of fate if we could help it. Everything possible was done to prevent the young gorillas meeting up with dangerous bugs. Special measures were taken against cockroaches, frequent visitors to animal houses which can carry poliomyelitis. Like children, Jo-Jo and Suzy also had polio vaccine on lumps of sugar. The

148

air into their sleeping quarters was filtered and treated with antifungal chemicals and their fruit and vegetables were washed to remove traces of any pesticide or other substance sprayed on by the grower. Len, their keeper, virtually lived with them in a small room near theirs in the ape house. There he would prepare their special diet, measure out their vitamin drops, boil their milk and slip in a nourishing egg, whip up their Ovaltine nightcap and select the ingredients for their broth from a larder plentifully stocked with vegetables of all kinds from asparagus to leeks, from string beans to back-eyed peas. Len also spent long periods playing with and nursing the little creatures; of course, a very important part of his job. Their games were simple and boisterous: playing tag, wrestling, somersaulting. The animals thrived and grew rapidly and our precautions seemed to work well. We had no infectious disease, just the development of Jo-Jo's migraine after some years and an allergic rash on his leg that broke out each year when the summer brought plant pollen into his open-air enclosure.

Jo-Jo soon grew into a powerful young juvenile who packed quite a punch when playing with humans. Suzy was gentler and more reticent but Jo-Jo liked nothing better than his daily roustabouts with Len, Matt Kelly or the zoo director, Mr Legge. His favourite wheeze was to saunter past one's legs, apparently intent on other business and ignoring one's presence, but as he drew level he would deliver a beefy clout to the kneecap with a flick of his hand and scurry off gleefully, looking back over his shoulder for the expected pursuit. The bigger he got the more the kneecaps, mine included, began to complain.

The gorillas loved being picked up and cuddled. This was easy when they weighed ten or twenty pounds but later we found the muscular, seventy-pound youngsters who insisted on being rocked in one's arms a bit more of a problem. The trouble was not the ache in the arms as the ape lay dozing cheek to cheek but the crucial point when the nursing and playing

149

had to stop until the next day. Like spoilt children Jo-Jo and Suzy objected petulantly to the humans leaving them to their own devices and would nip firmly at bits of the anatomy or seize hold of clothing with a vice-like grip. At first they were not big enough to enforce their point of view too vigorously, but as time went on this behaviour made inspections increasingly more tricky. I would go into their indoor quarters with Mr Legge and Len, the keeper. To have a good look at Jo-Jo's gums, to see whether his colour was satisfactory, to peer with an ophthalmoscope into his dark and sparkling eyes or listen to his chest with a stethoscope meant first playing the kneecap-knocking game and then, when I could stand no more, letting my playmate drape himself around me for a cuddle. When he was satisfactorily positioned in my arms with bits of him looped round my neck, poked into my ear or lovingly entangled with my hair, I would use a free arm if I had one, or someone else's if not, to remove the necessary instrument from my pocket and to place it surreptitiously on the appropriate spot. The examination over, I then had to rid myself of the gorilla which meant passing him to somebody else, usually Len. The gorillas did not mind being swapped in this way and seemed to think that one cuddler was as good as another. Len would then be the last to leave the quarters. After Mr Legge and I had gone Len would unpick the gorilla from his person and put it on the floor. As it began to protest and snatch for him again he would slip quickly out through the door.

That was how it was at first but as time went on Len did not always make it. He would find himself squeezing dexterously through the door into the passage with two, three or four shiny black arms re-attaching themselves to his clothing, limbs or hair. Increasingly he left bits behind and the rigmarole of breaking off the day's fun became longer and more complex. Came the day when the three of us were in the gorilla quarters for my routine medical inspection and Jo-Jo, now developing the auburn shock of hair on his forehead characteristic of a mature male and rippling his biceps like Mr Universe, decided on a showdown.

The examination on Jo-Jo went without any trouble. He clung to me with an innocent expression on his face and snuffled at my ear. Then it was time to leave him. As soon as I nonchalantly tried to set him down I felt his muscles tighten. He bared his teeth and lost his innocent look.

'You'd better have him as usual,' I told Len.

Len came alongside and Jo-Jo thought about it. OK, he was prepared to move across. Seventy pounds of warm and hairy gorilla slipped from my arms with movements like mercury and made itself comfortable round Len's upper half. As usual Mr Legge and I left the room and Len backed off towards the door. Once there he tried to unpick the ape, but as his fingers tried to release Jo-Jo's grip it either got tighter or simply rang the changes. As soon as he managed to free one hand from a hold on his shoulder, its place would be taken by a foot or, more menacingly, by a strong pair of jaws digging in not quite enough to break the skin but with a mouthful of flesh securely imprisoned. Len struggled and cajoled. Titbits of grapes and bananas and apricots were brought. Jo-Jo was not being bought off. If Len was leaving the room so was Jo-Jo and the gorilla seemed to be adamant that as far as he was concerned the Siamese-twin relationship would last forever.

'Let me have a go with him,' said Mr Legge. 'Perhaps he'll let me put him down. Anyway I'm perhaps a bit more nimble than you, Len.'

He went back in. Yes, Jo-Jo was quite happy about another change. The look of innocence returned to his face and he transferred his affections to the zoo director. Now it was Mr Legge's turn to move with his burden until he was just inside the door and then, cooing soothingly and stroking Jo-Jo's head with one hand, to try to loosen the ape's hold with his other hand. Jo-Jo pretended to be snoozing peacefully but his iron-hard black nails dug into Mr Legge's clothing with a sudden sharp movement. I swear he was peeping out between closed eyelids. Nothing doing. The gorilla stuck like a malevolent limpet. Half an hour went by and it was time to try another change. Matt Kelly was called in. Jo-Jo went to him like a lamb but when Matt tried to divest himself of the animal he lost some hair, a pocket and all the buttons from his shirt front. He did not lose the gorilla. I was in a quandary. Transferring the gorilla was easy but at this rate we would soon run out of gorilla holders or ape donees or whatever one likes to call them. Dope seemed to be the answer but using the dart-gun or giving tranquillising injections might stimulate Jo-Jo to take it out on the current holder before dropping to sleep, and gorillas can bite hard and rip viciously with their fingers. We would have to do it without the infliction of even a minute amount of pain, which meant that the only way to adminster the drug was by mouth. In the food store I injected a knock-out dose of phencyclidine into the pulp of a banana without actually peeling the fruit. Jo-Jo likes to peel his own.

Back in the ape house Matt was sitting glumly on the floor, almost totally submerged by the loving heap of gorilla that clasped him. There is a rule about giving doped bananas to apes or doctored sausages to wolves or hollowed-out loaves of bread containing medicine to suspicious hippopotamuses: always proffer first a sterling, pristine, untampered-with and impeccable article of the same kind. Having established your credentials with number one, you then emerge in your true colours by nobbling number two. With this in mind I offered a normal banana to Jo-Jo. He took it, peeled it with one hand and his teeth (the other hand was maintaining its hold on Matt's right ear), ate the pulp with relish, licked the skin and threw it down. Now I produced the Trojan horse, or rather the Trojan banana. Again Jo-Jo took it, peeled it and prepared to thrust it into his mouth. Then out of the recesses of his mind came either a generous thought or, more likely I suspect, an inkling, just an embryonic inkling, that malpractice was afoot. With a gentle pouting of his lips and a soothing cooing sound Jo-Jo rammed the fruit of the banana firmly between Matt's

152

lips. The head keeper spluttered and gulped but Jo-Jo was insistent that Matt was going to have his banana. I was horrified. If Matt swallowed the doctored banana pulp he would be unconscious within ten minutes and, worse, might suffer for days afterwards from the reported side effects of erotic fantasies and burning sensations in the extremities.

'Spit it out, for God's sake!' I shouted. 'Don't swallow any banana, Matt!'

Matt spat for dear life. Jo-Jo seemed distinctly surprised at the ingratitude and tried to poke bits of the mushed pulp back between Matt's teeth. Matt continued to puff out furiously, rolling his eyes at us as we stood watching helplessly. Suzy came over and helped clean up the mess. She picked the spat-out bits off Jo-Jo's hairy chest like a wife carefully sponging the soup stains off her husband's dinner jacket. Not a bit of the banana did Jo-Jo eat nor would he accept any further pieces of food. Eventually, for it was by now well on into the evening, it was decided to try to relieve poor Matt by doing yet another change, this time back to Len again. The transfer went smoothly but still Len could not get out of the room without his ape.

'I've heard of having a monkey on one's back,' he remarked glumly, 'but I've got a gorilla on my front!'

At last it was decided to leave Len in the gorilla quarters. A comfortable chair was brought in and a transistor radio was left playing outside the door. When Mr Legge went back at midnight Jo-Jo was still comfortably, immovably, in situ. Len tried to doze. It was seven o'clock the following morning before Jo-Jo finally fell into a deep, forgetful slumber and Len was able to lower him gently to the floor, to steal out of the room and lock up.

Never again did we go in with the two gorillas. When I needed to examine them I used the dart-gun and a tranquilliser. But we all remember affectionately the happy times we had playing tag with a pair of baby gorillas. Like children, it's a pity they have to grow up.

Fourteen

Of all the trips abroad on which my work has taken me, the one which may yet have the most far-reaching results came about when, after years of fruitless applications for a visa to visit China, I was eventually invited to spend two weeks studying animal acupuncture and inspecting zoological collections in that country. At that time few Western zoologists had been given the opportunity to see the Chinese animal collections, many of which contain species never exhibited in the West. I was anxious to see some of the very rare creatures that inhabit China's most inaccessible regions and to find out whether and to what degree the science of acupuncture was being applied to animals, particularly undomesticated ones.

With Gary Smart, one of the directors of the Royal Windsor Safari Park, I flew out to Peking. We arrived in bitterly cold weather, and in the middle of the night, at the forbidding, Stalinesque Peking airport, where we were met by Mr Lo, a delightful, slightly-built young man who was to be our guide, interpreter and political mentor. He told us we could go where we liked and photograph anything and explained that, although he had not handled a veterinary scientist before, he had carefully prepared a handwritten phrase book of words which might be needed by him during our discourses. It was crammed with every conceivable veterinary word from ana-plasmosis to Zonules of Zinn, each with the corresponding Chinese ideogram.

'That, Dr Taylor,' he said, smiling broadly, 'will come in useful when we go round the zoos and hospitals. But first, as a good friend of China, you will want to see our progress in light engineering, agricultural communes, heavy industry, textile production and so forth.'

We felt obliged to murmur our assent. For three days we inspected light-bulb factories and sheds where Peking ducks were force-fed by machines, we were sung to by infant schools and toured secondary schools where every class had some special item of entertainment ready for us, we looked at tractor exhibitions and blocks of flats, we had tea and sweets with little old ladies who told us how cruel landlords used to be, and we drank gallons of delightful green tea with innumerable revolutionary committees, each member of which described a particular aspect of progress in birth control, the manufacture of bricks, shipbuilding or the eradication of all traces of Confucianism. But not a zoo, not a wolf nor a snake, not a monkey nor a panda did we see. We became increasingly anxious that the continuous socio-political hurly-burly might take up the whole of our visit. Then, far more pleasantly, began a series of visits to the great and glorious relics of the old China, the Forbidden City, the great wall, the Ming tombs and palaces, temples, monasteries and gardens. It was all immensely fascinating, but still we saw no zoos. At last, our patience wearing if not thin at least somewhat slimmer, we felt that we had served our apprenticeship in Anglo-Chinese friendship and made forceful representations to be shown the things that we had paid many hundreds of pounds to come and see. At last we set foot in our first Chinese zoo park, in Peking.

The zoo was stuffed with animals and birds that we had never seen before. There were giant Tibetan donkeys, the most dangerous animals in the zoo, we were told, when they are in the mating season. A north-east Chinese tiger far outstripped the record size given in the *Guinness Book of Records*. There were reptiles and birds found only in remote corners of that vast country, and elephants and rhinoceros only recently discovered in their own Chinese forests. We spent a long time admiring the fabulous golden monkeys from the snow-

155

covered north. These unique primates with bright blue faces, snub noses and long golden hair were the most handsome monkeys I have ever seen. Then there were the giant pandas, an adorable group of youngsters lying on their backs in the sun chewing sugar cane and bamboo.

All the animals seemed very healthy and contented but when at the end of our tour of the zoo we had the usual formal meeting with the revolutionary committee that runs it, I could find out little about their veterinary services. They declined to show us the veterinary laboratory as being unworthy and inadequate and they said that acupuncture was never used on the zoo stock. I asked for samples from the giant pandas, which I was keen to examine for parasites. There was always the chance that one would find some new and unnamed species of worm or fluke in the droppings of so rare a creature. Plastic bags full of droppings from each of the pandas were promptly produced. At the end of my visit I carefully carried them back to England, only to find on detailed microscopical examination that not one of the samples contained any sign of a single unwanted guest. My daydreams of being remembered by posterity through some obscure maggot bearing my latinised name were dashed.

After Peking we visited Shanghai and Canton zoos. At each the picture was the same – a priceless stock of mainly Chinese animals, a polite but firm refusal to give information on medical care, and a complete lack of interest in buying from or exchanging animals with the West. As for selling animals to European zoos it was politely explained that as the stock belonged to the people only the people could give permission. It was not altogether clear how the people went about voicing their opinions. No-one cared to comment on the pandas given to certain Western heads of state nor on the sensible exchanges of animals which had recently taken place with Whipsnade Zoo in England.

I was determined to see acupuncture being practised and insisted that Mr Lo should organise it, since I was being frustrated in the primary aim of my Chinese trip. First we were shown dental clinics where patients sat in long rows of chairs receiving routine attention to their mouths. Some had opted for what we would call orthodox local anaesthetic injections to numb the pain. Others were receiving treatment under acupuncture anaesthesia, and these patients had one or two fine stainless steel wires protruding from their hands or arms. Next we were taken to an outpatients' clinic where minor ailments such as headache, lumbago and muscle sprains were being dealt with. In a small room we found a crowd of people of both sexes, standing, sitting or lying on benches. They positively sprouted needles all over the place, from heads, necks, arms, backs, legs and toes. Not a drop of blood could be seen oozing anywhere. Later I saw a baby delivered and a lung lobe removed using the same techniques. In each case the patient was conscious and able to talk with the surgeons during the operation. But I still had to see acupuncture used on animals.

One day Mr Lo arrived at our hotel to say that I was invited to the Central Veterinary Clinic in Peking, where an operation had been laid on. We drove out to the clinic, a complex of single-storey buildings covered in anti-revisionist slogans. The revolutionary committee of veterinarians welcomed us with the usual tea party and hour of political instruction before we got down to business. It was explained that although they used acupuncture anaesthesia in around 200 major operations on cattle, horses and mules each year, they had not got any large animal needing surgery on the day of my visit. To my dismay, although I must admit I felt unwilling to try and stop them, they proposed to operate on a perfectly healthy old horse and remove a piece of its large intestine.

First they gave me a carefully prepared lecture, illustrated with pictures pinned up on the wall, on the precise anatomical landmarks used for finding the correct acupuncture spot for each operation. It appeared that the clinic was using the method as a matter of routine for surgery of the head, chest

157

and abdomen, although they reported only fair results in removing sensation from the limbs below the elbow or knee. Research, they said, was continuing into animal acupuncture anaesthesia: the operation that I would see that day would need only two needles, whereas a year before they would have had to use fourteen for the same job. Research and refinement of the technique for locating the needle points precisely by using a sort of galvanometer that detects changes in the electrical resistance of the skin at these points, together with the diligent application of Chairman Mao's thoughts, had rendered twelve needles redundant.

We went into a rather odd operating theatre that resembled a Pennine cow byre and all donned white gowns, caps and masks. The place was poorly equipped and badly in need of painting but they did have a useful-looking, hydraulically operated large-animal operating table. A tired old grey mare was led in. She was hobbled to the table in the verticle position and when secure was gently revolved until she was lying on her side. The anaesthetist produced two long acupuncture needles which had been sterilising in a pan boiling away on a gas ring and indicated the points which had been described in my briefing. For complete anaesthesia of the left side of the horse's abdomen and bowels she was going to put one needle into the leg foreleg above the knee and the other into the same leg but below the knee. Swabbing the chosen sites with alcohol, she pressed the needles in. The one above the knee was pressed diagonally downwards through the flesh until it had almost transfixed the limb and was tenting the skin on the inside of the leg. Mr Lo moaned as he stood beside me.

'Dr Taylor, I am going to be sick,' he said, turning away. He was certainly going green above his mask.

For the horse the insertion of the needle was probably no more painful than having a deep shot of local anaesthetic and it lay calmly enough. When the needles were exactly in position wires from an alternating current generator were clipped to them. Knobs were turned and dials were set on the machine.

Small muscles in the leg near the acupuncture needles began to twitch and flicker.

'Now we wait for ten minutes,' said the anaesthetist. 'Then the surgeon can begin.'

Ten minutes passed. The horse lay blinking and supping water through a tube from a kettle. The foreleg muscles continued to twitch but otherwise there was nothing to suggest that the animal was anything but totally conscious and in command of all its senses. The surgeon picked up his scalpel. I clenched my fists under my gown. He was going to have to open the flank for a good twelve inches in one continuous incision biting deep through skin and fat. Rather you than me, old boy, I thought. It was impossible to conceive that those two needles and the electric box buzzing away by the horse's head could have removed all feeling of pain from an apparently unrelated area several feet away. Nothing I had learnt in those long days at university in Glasgow, taking formaldehyde-pickled horse corpses to bits under the eagle eye of the anatomy tutor, had suggested any link between the foreleg and the belly. I was a prisoner of my Western training. What do we really know about the nervous system, particularly the elusive network that we call the autonomic? I was to come to believe that it was in this microscopic infrastructure of communication and command that the secret of acupuncture lay.

The scalpel pressed down onto the flesh and with a single elegant stroke the horse's side was unzipped down to the muscle layers. It did not bat an eyelid. I was watching intently for any sign of tensing or other reaction to the sudden pain of the knife, but there was nothing. The surgeon deftly opened the muscle, then sliced through the most sensitive layer of all, the peritoneum. A horse's peritoneum is thick and jam-packed with nerve endings. Surely now the old grey would wince or struggle? No, it just supped on at its kettle.

The loops of intestine were now visible. The surgeon pulled gently and then vigorously on a loop. Oddly enough, the bowel and its attachments have no nerve endings that can

159

detect cutting or even burning, but they do contain lots of endings that scream blue murder at the slightest tugging, stretching or twisting. That is why horses suffer such pain from the griping distensions and distortions of the bowel in colic, pain that can literally shock them to death. This old grey seemed totally oblivious to the pulling. Expertly the surgeon took out a portion of the bowel wall and stiched up the incision, then smoothly and rapidly he closed the various layers of the operation wound. Half an hour later the skin was closed. The anaesthetists switched off the electric machine and withdrew the needles. The table was returned to an upright position and the old horse was released. Steady as a rock, and dropping a healthy pile of manure on the way, she walked outside into the yard and began to eat corn heartily from a trough. I was most impressed.

Over the next few days I spent as much time as I could with the vets at the clinic. They had no experience of working with zoo animals, and as dogs and cats are regarded as unproductive creatures and are rarely seen in China (they are as rare as flies, which have been almost completely eradicated in China; during two weeks in the country we saw no dogs, one cat and two flies) they could give no advice about using acupuncture on carnivores. However, charts of the acupuncture points on horses, cattle and humans, together with sets of needles and even little plastic men and animals on which to practise, are widely and cheaply available throughout China. The man in the street and the 'barefoot doctors', the medical auxiliary workers who go into the countryside to take medical attention to the peasants and the peasants' animals, are encouraged to become proficient in this cheap and highly portable means of wide-ranging therapy.

China convinced me that there is a place in Western medicine for the development of acupunture. If I worked with small animals such as dogs and cats, I would experiment with the needles on certain conditions which are still difficult to tackle thoroughly by orthodox methods. Nervous diseases, fits,

160

paralysis, arthritic conditions and skin diseases seem ideal areas for investigation. But how to use the technique on my patients, the zoo animals? By studying the charts of the cow and the horse and the man which I had brought back from China, together with the set of 'barefoot doctor' needles and a small electric machine, I realised that the needle insertion point which treats a specific type of disease or produces anaesthesia of a particular area is in the same corresponding anatomical position in each of the three species. For example the point on the human hand between the base of the thumb and the index finger, which affects the teeth, is anatomically identical to the position of the outside of the cow's foot or on the top of the horse's cannon bone which affects the teeth in those species. In difficult cases which were not yielding to conventional treatment I would try transposing the acupuncture points of the horse, cow or man onto my zoo animal patients. It would be difficult with uniquely shaped animals like dolphins, and I have since learned that American vets have so far had no luck in identifying the acupuncture areas in these creatures. Still, the striking improvement in many cases of dolphin disease where the animal has been pricked with injection needles carrying perhaps only vitamin shots suggests that it is not always the medication that does the trick but that unwittingly the hypodermics may have hit the bullseye on an acupuncture point.

Shortly after returning from China I had my first suitable case for acupuncture. Eddie, a young giraffe at Royal Windsor Safari Park, had been dogged with chronic recurring arthritis of all four ankle joints ever since he had damaged the joints repeatedly during a rough passage through the Bay of Biscay on his way to Britain as a baby. Eddie's joints were a mess – enlarged, thickened with scar tissue round the joint capsule and prone to flare up frequently into a painful, laming, inflammatory condition. He had had all sorts of treatment from poultices and cortisone to courses of gold and new anti-arthritic drugs. Nothing worked for long. I decided to give Eddie five twenty-minute courses of acupuncture at weekly intervals, using the points on his body anatomically equivalent to the ones which the Chinese used for polyarthritis in cattle.

Eddie was enticed by succulent oak branches into a restraining pen where he was unable to turn round or back away. With the aid of a ladder I climbed up the side of the pen and selected the two points over the rib-cage which I hoped would do the trick. I disinfected the skin and pushed the thin needles in about one inch deep. Eddie did not seem to care: he was used to injections and these needles were far finer than the ones used for administering drugs. I clipped on the two wires leading to the generator which was powered by a tiny transistor radio battery. Tense with anticipation I turned on the control switch. A little red light began to flash in the box. I adjusted the frequency control according to the instructions I had received in China, and the superficial muscles in the skin between the two needles began to twitch. Eddie continued to munch oak leaves. Twenty minutes later I switched off, withdrew the needles and climbed down the ladder. Eddie limped away.

The giraffe's condition appeared unchanged, but three days later the giraffe keeper reported a definite improvement in Eddie's gait. I was not prepared to hope that it was because of the acupuncture. One week later I repeated the treatment. Eddie was undoubtedly walking much better and I had a sneaking suspicion that his joints were not quite so grotesquely enlarged. The next week I was certain. Eddie's joints were on the mend. By the time the course of treatments was complete the giraffe's joints were almost down to normal size, better than we had ever seen them since he had arrived, and he walked gracefully without a trace of a limp. Now the question was whether the arthritis would relapse after a time just as it had done following all the other forms of therapy. We waited. One, two, three weeks went by. Two months passed and still Eddie's joints were holding up. He had never been sound for so long. After four months we decided that it was fair to claim that he had made a remarkable recovery quite different from the temporary improvements seen in the past.

It left me itching to try the technique on some more knotty cases in exotic animals, but my second acupuncture patient turned out to be my elder daughter, Stephanie. Going home one evening I found her miserably complaining of toothache. Remembering the dental clinic I had seen in China and the ease with which the acupuncturists had numbed the teeth via a readily locatable point on the hand, I prevailed upon her to let me use my magic box and needle on her. Reluctantly, but remembering my frequent enthusiastic progress reports on Eddie, she agreed. Two minutes after I had popped in the needle she announced that the toothache had gone. Whatever the explanation of the mechanism behind acupuncture, I admit that in her case suggestion may have played an important part. But when I see Eddie cantering in the sunlight with that fluid motion so charming and so typical of giraffes, his ankles slim and free from ugly knobbles, I am certain that nobody suggested anything to him.

If you have enjoyed reading this book you will be interested to know that three other books by David Taylor are published by Unwin Paperbacks.